Cinnamon Simpson

Jarvis Clutch—Social Spy

by

Dr. Mel Levine and Jarvis Clutch

Illustrations by Ed Shems

Educators Publishing Service
Cambridge and Toronto

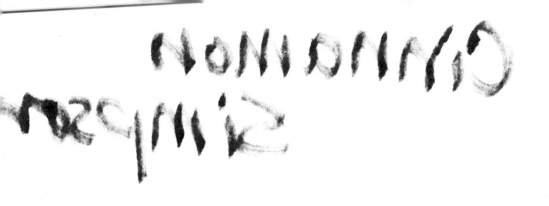

Educators Publishing Service
A division of Delta Education, LLC
800.225.5750
www.epsbooks.com

Illustrations by Ed Shems
Design by Persis Barron Levy
Editor: Stacey L. Nichols
Managing Editor: Sheila Neylon

Printed in U.S.A.
ISBN 0-8388-2620-2
04 05 06 07 08 CUR 07 06 05 04 03

This book is dedicated to students who too often have felt the horrible pain of isolation or humiliation—in the hope that these pages will equip them with the insights they need to experience healthy and happy social lives.

THANK YOU VERY MUCH....

Jarvis and Dr. Levine would like to thank a whole bunch of great people who helped them with *Jarvis Clutch—Social Spy.*

First, they want to thank nine students from different parts of the United States who read an early version of the book and made lots of good suggestions. The student reviewers were Jarrett Barnhill III, Benjamin Case, Natalie Case, Krysta Frye, Allison Gay, Caitlin McDevitt, David Menich, Amy Middleton, and Will Pierce. Also, they want to extend their appreciation to Andrew Dismukes, a summer intern at All Kinds of Minds. He helped them understand the social scene based on his own experiences in school, and was especially helpful in clueing us into what kids talk about at parties! They would also like to thank Dr. Bob Brooks, who is Dr. Levine's very good friend and a famous and brilliant child psychologist. He read a draft of *Jarvis Clutch—Social Spy* and suggested some important changes.

Stacey Nichols was this book's number one editor at Educators Publishing Service. She was super at fixing all kinds of mistakes, and she came up with lots of ways to make this a much better book. Pam McBain, Dr. Levine's assistant, helped out with pulling things together, and Dr. Levine's wife, Bambi (Jarvis isn't married yet), gave us some great ideas, too. She also graciously put up with Dr. Levine as he spent many long hours plugging away at *Jarvis Clutch—Social Spy.*

Additionally, Dr. Levine would like to thank Charles Schwab and the rest of the board of All Kinds of Minds for their continuing support, passion, superb guidance, and inspiration. Dr. Levine is also grateful to the Maternal and Child Health Bureau (through its LEND grant program) and the Administration for Developmental Disabilities, both of which are United States government agencies that help to fund the Clinical Center for the Study of Development and Learning at the University of North Carolina.

ABOUT DR. MEL LEVINE

Dr. Mel Levine is a pediatrician, a kid's doctor. He decided to become a doctor when he was only eight years old, although he also thought about being a veterinarian because he loves animals. Dr. Levine now lives on Sanctuary Farm in North Carolina, where he raises mostly geese, about 240 of them in all. Many of his birds are very rare and beautiful. He also loves and breeds mammoth donkeys, swans, pheasants, peacocks, Great Danes, German shepherds, and Maine coon cats on his farm. Many of his donkeys and geese have real trouble with their social cognition, but they're all right. Dr. Levine says that when he goes into one of his goose pens, he feels as if he is in the corridor of a middle school. That's because he sees a lot of macho geese displaying for each other and trying to act as cool as possible to impress their bird peers.

For many years, Dr. Levine has been interested in kids in school, especially how they learn and the ways in which they can become successful in life. He is especially interested in students who have a hard time in school even though they're really smart. He tries to help those kids turn their lives around and discover what it feels like to do well in school. He strongly believes that every mind has great strengths and ways to accomplish fantastic things; it's just a matter of figuring out how to get it going in the right direction. Dr. Levine also deals with kids who are having a hard time on the social scene, which is why he wrote this book.

Dr. Levine is a Professor of Pediatrics at the University of North Carolina in Chapel Hill. There, he is the director of the Clinical Center for the Study of Development and Learning, which studies different kinds of learning problems that kids have and trains people to understand and help kids who are struggling in school and in their social lives. He also directs All Kinds of Minds, an institute that offers new ways to help parents, teachers, and kids deal with differences in learning and become successful in life. If you want to learn more about All Kinds of Minds and its work, you can visit their Web site at www.allkindsofminds.org.

Dr. Levine has written many books and articles. Three of his books, *Keeping a Head in School, All Kinds of Minds,* and *The Language Parts Cataolg,* are written for kids to help them understand their own ways of learning, thinking, and behaving. *Jarvis Clutch—Social Spy* is Dr. Levine's fourth kid's book.

Dr. Levine always did pretty well in school, but he had trouble with sports. Also, kids used to make fun of his first name (Melvin), and they sometimes humiliated him in physical education classes. Mostly, Dr. Levine was a loner. He liked being by himself—and he still does. He doesn't much like big parties and big events (like basketball games). He is a little eccentric. For example, most of his friends don't raise geese—they play golf, go fishing or hunting, and attend dances instead. Although he does have good friends and likes being with people, Dr. Levine is not a conformist. He tries very hard to be his true self.

~ ABOUT JARVIS CLUTCH ~

Jarvis Clutch is like Dr. Levine in some important ways. But he is also his own unique person. If you want to know more about Jarvis, you can read about his life in Chapter 6 of this book.

~

~ CHAPTER 1 ~
I'M JARVIS CLUTCH

Hi. I'm Jarvis Clutch. I know that's a weird name. Don't go after me, reader. I didn't pick it out, but sometimes I get picked on because of it. Anyway, I'm supposed to be writing this book about school—just about the social part of school. Dr. Mel Levine, my doctor, is writing it with me. You see, I was required (that means forced) to do a project for school with some grown-up I know. So I picked Dr. Levine. Lucky for him. He's very interested in kids my age and how they learn and how they get along. Maybe he was willing to help me because he thinks I *can't* learn and *don't* get along very well with other kids! Just kidding. It was his big idea that for this project I should spend a few months checking out the social scene here at school. I was supposed to watch how kids in my middle school act, talk, and try to come across when they're with each other. And I was supposed to notice kids who were good at making friends and kids who were especially talented at making enemies without really trying—a very interesting skill. So I did what I had to do. I took notes (lots of which I couldn't read afterward) and I recorded a few conversations. Some of them came out OK and others were useless because I forgot to change the dumb batteries in the Stone Age cassette recorder that my mom lent me. I think it originally belonged to her grandmother, who had gotten it from *her* grandmother!

I had to look over all the stuff I collected, and then I went through that well-known cruel and unusual torture for innocent, suffering middle school kids: I had to write a report, which is not a favorite form of thrilling entertainment for your average guy my age. But I did it. With Dr. Levine's very, very kind and mostly hassling, Jarvis-bugging assistance, I wrote the report, thirty-two pages of Jarvis talking about the social scene. And guess what, reader? I got an A on my report, an A for absolutely astonishing and amazingly axcellent (I've never been much of a speller). This might not seem so unbelievably dazzling and thrilling to you, but I swear to you that in my life, As have been about as common as five feet of snow in the middle of the summer! But then, get this: because I got that stupid A and was so excellent at observing and talking about other kids, Dr. Levine suggested that we take all the stuff I found out, try to get even more inside dirt, and write a book together! That sounded like the worst idea I had heard in the entire fourteen years of my life (I'm not sure what I heard inside my mom). Yes, I was going to be brutally punished and abused for getting an A on a report by having to write more! You see, I learned that success can cost you something. But after a lot of hassling, I agreed to do it. So, reader, you are now reading the book that Dr. Levine and I wrote together.

MY SOCIAL SPYING

Here's how it worked: I wrote about different kids, taken from real, teenage human-animal-type life in the Eastern Middle School jungle. Each chapter talks about a different part of how kids try to get along with each other. At certain moments during my very accurate and mostly useless descriptions, Dr. Levine jumps in (interrupts) with mostly very intelligent things to say in order to teach us all something and impress us with all the great stuff he knows. He sometimes shows us some weird diagrams that he designed to help us understand, or to make sure we're completely confused, about the whole world of social life. He makes up these diagrams when he has nothing better to do. He says that they help kids who like to learn things visually. Sometimes in my parts of the chapter, I might say some things about what he had to say about what I said. At the end of each chapter, Dr. Levine makes comments and then we ask some questions that you, the loving, fascinated reading public, are supposed to think about and maybe discuss with your friends or classmates if you feel like it (or if someone forces you to). Or, you could always talk to some strangers or your pet ant colony or a hermit crab instead. You could even talk to yourself if you and yourself get along OK. I also came up with some writing and spying projects that you can do if you don't have a more interesting way to spend your time.

SOME SURPRISINGLY BORING STUFF ABOUT ME

Let me begin this fascinating book by filling you in on a few unimportant and boring personal things about me that are basically none of your business. As you know, I happen to be Jarvis Clutch. I'm fourteen, and I'm a prisoner in eighth grade at Eastern Middle School, which I hate. I can't stand the place. The work kills, there are too many teachers (and some of them are really hard to understand), and there are a lot of kids I don't like much and about the same number who would not want to join any Jarvis fan club, for sure. I mean some kids are actually totally mean. In a way, I'm one of them. I mean, I'm mean too—at least sometimes in some ways. I've been known to join in making fun of kids for things they can't help. At least I realize how mean that is right after I do it, so then I cool it.

In case you're wondering, Eastern Middle School was given its very clever name to make sure people didn't go to Western Middle School by mistake. Last year they built a third middle school, which I wanted them to name Middle Middle School. Because it was the smallest middle school in town, I thought they could even call it Little Middle Middle School. When it was being built, there was all this steel stuff they put up, and I told someone that they needed to call it Metal Middle Middle School. But the people who run our schools, known throughout the world for their hilarious sense of humor and originality, decided to call it Central Middle School. No one ever listens to Jarvis.

As you may have decided already, I'm actually pretty creative and I have a decent sense of humor, more than most kids. I'm fairly good at writing stories and things, and I like to use writing to make fun of stuff and people. But I'll warn you, I can't spell, and my handwriting is not even as neat as what an elephant could get on paper writing with its trunk. Dr. Levine says we're having an editor, someone who looks everything over and fixes up the spelling and grammar, double-check this book before it gets printed. Good thing! I may start asking that person to check all of my homework! Also, my reading public, you're in luck: you don't have to try to decipher my handwriting, because I'm using a computer, the one my older brother used to use before he got a good one. I call my computer "the scraptop" because it's such a piece of junk that it should really go straight to the trash heap.

DR. LEVINE'S IDEAS

Now, for the great moment that you haven't been waiting for! We're going to hear from Dr. Mel Levine, my always very interested and sometimes even a little bit interesting writing partner. By the way, he says it's OK if I just call him Levine or else Dr. Mel or Dr L.—he doesn't care, I guess, as long as I say ridiculously nice stuff about him, even if I don't completely mean it.

So now let's meet and greet Dr. Mel Levine, who is here to teach you about a very major main idea in this very major fabulous book.

• SOMETHING CALLED SOCIAL COGNITION •

Thanks, Jarvis. It's great to be writing this book with Jarvis Clutch. As you will discover, he is a very special kid, and there are parts of Jarvis that are inside all of us.

Jarvis Clutch—Social Spy is mainly about something very important called *social cognition,* which most likely is a term you've never heard before, even though it's something you use all day long. Even most grown-ups don't know exactly what it means. Let me explain. We all know that *thinking* is using your mind for something, such as trying to understand math, fixing a computer, learning a foreign language, or imagining an original story. Well, *cognition* is just another word for thinking. So, *social cognition* is just thinking about social things. It's the use of your mind to form and keep up good relationships with other people. You use your social cognition to make friends and stay on good terms with them. You use your social cognition to understand other people when they're with you, by asking yourself questions like "Does that person like me or not? Why is she saying that to me? Why is he acting this way with me?" Social cognition also helps you seem right, talk right, and act right when you're with other people. We'll explain more about those three things in the next few chapters of this book.

• • •

Here we can see how social cognition is affected by how much potential social ability people have when first born and how much they pick up along the way from different social experiences in school, in the neighborhood, at home, and in other places.

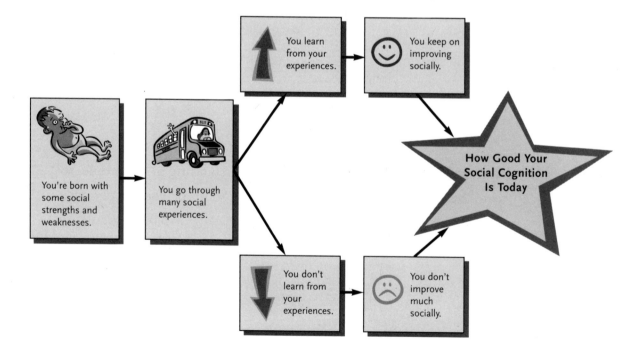

People get their social cognition in two ways. First, there are some parts of social cognition that you are definitely born with. Just as some people are born with the brain wiring to become great at sports, math, or art, some are born with the kind of mind that has great *people skills* that will just come out as they go through their school years. There are many students who have trouble doing well on their report cards and exams but have terrific social success, while others may be brainy students who have lots of social problems they can't solve. For example, they may have no friends or be very unpopular at school. Just as with all other abilities, some kids are excellent at social cognition, some are just OK or pretty fair social thinkers, and others seem to have too little social cognition to get along well. For these kids, social ability is a kind of disability—and it's not their fault, it's just the way their brains are wired. You have to feel sorry for those kids, and there are plenty of them.

Then there are some parts of social cognition that you learn as you go through life and pick up social experience over the years. You find out what works socially and what usually gets you into social difficulty (so you don't do that again). For example, you might spend a whole lunch hour boasting about how well you did in math and what a great soccer player you are, and then notice that no one wants to sit with you at lunch the next day. As a result, you add to your social cognition the knowledge that other people don't want to be with you if you keep trying to brag or boast too much when you're with them. You keep getting better at understanding other people, so you can form stronger relationships with them. Some of your experience comes from the culture you grow up in and from your own family and its values. Different cultures have their special forms of friendship and other relationships. Some families are more sociable and more interested in social life than others. All of that definitely rubs off on a kid.

So, learning and experience combine with your basic inborn social brain wiring to determine how successful and satisfied you will be on the social scene. As you move through life, you also learn just how social you are (or aren't). Different kids seem to want different amounts and types of social experience in their lives. That's for you to decide. Some kids want to be very popular or spend as much time as they can with friends, while others enjoy being by themselves a great deal.

For most people, social cognition decisions take place very quickly. You don't have to spend a long time figuring out what to say to people so that they won't think you're strange. When you are with other people, you might not even realize that the social part of your brain is actually working very hard so that you can get along well. If you have strong social cognition, most of that work takes place nearly automatically, meaning that you don't have to think about it all the time!

No matter how much and what type of social experience is right for you, social cognition is tremendously important. Not only does it help you make and keep friends, but you also need it for just about any career you can think of. If you want to succeed, you need to be able to get along well with the people you work with—and also with your supervisors or bosses. As a student, your social cognition can affect your performance in school, because it influences how well you get along with your teachers and classmates. For kids who are struggling with their social cognition, social situations are difficult, and this often makes them very unhappy. They may have trouble with friendships and sometimes they are picked on or made fun of by others. They may be forced to spend a lot of time alone, not because they want to, but because they have trouble finding friends and relating to other kids. So, you can see how having strong social cognition can make your life a lot easier.

A HARD TIME OF (SOCIAL) LIFE

Students in late elementary school and on into middle school and high school have to spend a lot of time and energy on social issues, matters that have very little to do with actual schoolwork or jobs. Middle school can be especially rough socially. That's why I asked Jarvis to write this book with me. Middle school students are right in the thick of the social struggle. This is a time when all kids have to think hard about who they are and how they fit in. It is a time when everyone is developing the part of his or her life that takes place outside of the family and outside of the classroom. This is also a time when kids can be pretty mean to each other, when they keep testing and sometimes teasing each other, and when they decide which kids to include and which ones will get excluded by various *social groups*. It can be very rough and painful, so it is especially important for middle school students to understand what is going on and to have some insight into their own social cognition and how it is working for or against them.

One way to start improving social cognition and getting in control of it in your life is to understand it. As you will see, social cognition has many different parts, which we will be explaining in this book. As you discover these parts of social cognition, you can be thinking about your relationships with other people and how these are being affected by your own social cognition abilities at this time in your life.

MORE ABOUT JARVIS CLUTCH

Before we start looking closely at the social scene and social cognition, I want to tell you a few more things about Jarvis Clutch. I think he's a great kid. But you should know that he's led a pretty hard life. You see, Jarvis's dad left home when Jarvis was only four, and no one has seen him since then. Some people think he had another woman or was in trouble with the law and left the country. But nobody knows for sure. Jarvis thinks about his father a lot, even though he can hardly remember what he looks like (except that Jarvis's mom has said that he looks a lot like his dad). Life without Mr. Clutch has been difficult for Mrs. Clutch, Jarvis, and Jarvis's older brother Jeremy. Mrs. Clutch has had to work extra hard and put in long hours to support her family, but she has done very well at providing for herself and her kids on her own. Over the years, Mrs. Clutch has been very proud of Jeremy, who gets fantastic grades, is a remarkable athlete, and is one of the most popular kids in his tenth grade class. She doesn't get to boast much about Jarvis, who has some problems in school, hates sports, and spends a lot of time all by himself. Maybe it's all that time alone that has made Jarvis a keen observer of other people. As you are about to find out, that's a real talent for him.

BECOMING AND STAYING SOCIALLY ACCEPTED: FIVE BIG SOCIAL CATEGORIES

I've said enough about Jarvis, at least for now. Let's go back and mention some things about the social scene, the part of Eastern Middle School Jarvis has been observing and writing about. We all know that all kids want to be accepted by other kids. That's only natural. No one wants to be on the outside all the time, rejected, bullied, or made fun of by others. That's where social cognition comes into play. It takes plenty of this ability to make and keep friends.

To better understand how kids fit in with each other, you can divide the students in any school into five different social categories. A category includes people who have some important things in common. The five social categories in any school are:

Popular kids are the ones just about everyone knows. They have excellent *reputations* and are liked and respected by large numbers of students. They get invited to plenty of parties. Lots of kids want to be with them. They seem to do everything right when it comes to getting accepted socially.

Fairly likable kids are students that are generally well-liked, but you wouldn't call them popular. They're mostly nice but are not as well-known as popular kids.

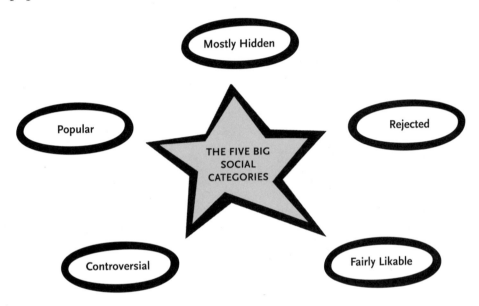

Controversial kids are popular with some students but quite unpopular with others. They may be part of a group of kids that stick together but are not really accepted by other groups. They are a kind of social minority within a school.

Mostly hidden kids are students no one knows well at all. They may seem to fade into the walls at school. There's nothing really wrong with them, but they're inconspicuous and they mind their own business. Very few people know them. Some are that way on purpose. They like being by themselves or maybe they don't completely approve of the other kids at school. Others don't try to be hidden, they just are, and nobody knows why. Maybe they're shy.

Rejected kids are usually miserable. They almost never get phone calls at home. Often they are excluded from activities, picked last for teams, forced to have lunch alone, or have to sit by themselves on the school bus. Sometimes other kids are downright cruel to them. They may get called names, and sometimes they are even physically harmed by bullies. In fact, some popular students may actually try to increase their power and popularity by picking on a rejected student.

One thing to remember about these groups is that kids in a particular group don't have to remain in that group. Over the years in school, they can move around from one group to another. A popular kid can become a loner or a rejected student can find a way to become popular. That happens. Also, if you fall within a category, it doesn't mean you just hang around all the time with kids in the same category. Some groups of friends contain kids from several different categories, although there is a tendency for the popular kids to want to stay together and for controversial students to try to be with groups of other controversial kids.

Does this sound right to you, Jarvis?

JARVIS'S THOUGHTS ON THE FIVE BIG SOCIAL CATEGORIES

I think Levine's mostly right on. We have those exact categories at Eastern Middle School. By now you might be wondering how to get into the popular category or how to make totally sure you don't totally collapse socially and become a poor, pathetic, suffering rejected kid. Well, I'm going to let you know. Believe it or not, that's what this whole book is about. It's about how kids make it or don't make it on the social battlefields of school. Also, in case you're wondering which category Jarvis Clutch is in, I'm not about to tell you—at least not yet. Try to guess.

Now let's get going and take our front-row seats at the major sporting event called "Social Cognition in Action at Eastern Middle School," a fierce game involving all the things you need to do to be as popular as you want to be and also what you need to do to make and keep your friends. Dr. Levine talked me into splitting social cognition into four parts: fitting in (and feeling good about it), seeming right, talking right, and acting right. To illustrate how all those ideas fit together, he made this mostly useless diagram:

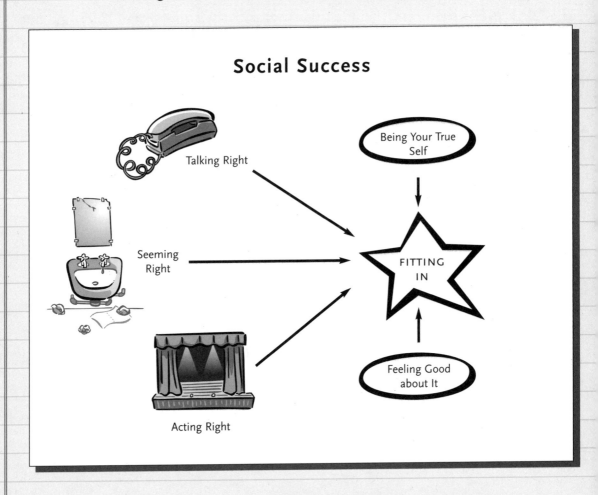

This diagram illustrates the next four chapters of this book, which talk about how seeming right, talking right, and acting right help determine if a kid will be socially successful. To start off, of course, kids have to feel good about the way they are fitting in (or maybe even not fitting in) and, at the same time, being a real person. What I mean is that kids have to find a way to fit in without having to be phonies, fakes, or kids who put on acts just so others will like them. Being your true self and fitting in can sometimes be really hard—as we will see in Chapter 2.

In Chapter 2, you will find out about the way kids try to fit in with each other or else find themselves on the outer edges of the social planet. You'll find out what I found out when I checked up on all the different abilities and attitudes that have to do with fitting in. Chapter 2 will change the way you think about the social scene at your school. You'll want to read it over and over as fast as you possibly can. So be prepared for the most exciting reading you have done in the last month, or at least in the last ten minutes!

But hold on. Before we have a ball reading Chapter 2, we're supposed to slow down (but not dumb down) our excellent brains and think and talk some more about what we learned in Chapter 1. I don't know if you were paying attention or not, but as I mentioned before, at the very end of each chapter of this brilliant book of ours, Dr. Levine and I (mostly him) have included some questions. You're supposed to look them over to find a few things to talk about or write about or worry about, or even get excited about. But please don't race away too fast because I also have a special treat in store for you. I, the one and only Jarvis Clutch, have included a couple of projects that I (not Dr. Levine) have thought up for you to do. They're especially helpful if you can't find anything better to do with your time. I hope everyone who reads this book will try one or two of my wildly thrilling Jarvis projects.

SOME SOCIAL QUESTIONS AND PROJECTS FROM THIS CHAPTER TO THINK ABOUT, DO, AND/OR DISCUSS

1. In your own words, what exactly is social cognition? Why do you think social cognition plays an important role in everyone's daily life?

2. What advantages do people have when they excel at social cognition?

3. Is social cognition something that people have to think about all of the time, some of the time, or never? Do you think that the way you act socially usually happens automatically, or do people have to plan out all of their social moves?

4. It has been said that middle school and the early teenage years require a lot of serious social cognition. What is it about this time of life that puts such a strain on social cognition?

5. Are kids in middle school very different in their social behavior from those in elementary school? If so, how?

6. How do you think that Jarvis's home life affects his social cognition?

7. Do the Five Big Social Categories (pages 18–20) exist in your school? Thinking about your school, are there any categories you might want to add to the list or subtract from it?

8. Is it easy for you to put yourself in one of these categories? If so, which one would you fit in the best? Why? Could you fit most other students at your school into one of the categories?

9. What is it about certain kids that gets them into the rejected category? Is it their fault that they are in this category?

10. Have you seen kids change from one category to another as they go through school? If so, how does this happen? Do they change or do others change their feelings about them?

11. Are there any things in this chapter that really are not true at your school? What are they?

★ JARVIS PROJECT FOR CHAPTER 1 ★

Writing/Drawing Project: Write a story about a controversial kid or else draw a cartoon showing a boy or girl who is controversial. Try to show why that kid is well liked by some students and treated like he or she has some kind of virus by others.

~ CHAPTER 2 ~

FITTING IN AND FEELING GOOD ABOUT IT

The chapter you are about to try to get through (or get over with) is all about fitting in. You see, I have found (with the very trusty and sometimes kinda rusty not-too-helpful help of Dr. Levine) that feeling right about the social side of your life is all about finding a way of fitting in in a way you feel good about. This way has to work just right for you, even though it may not be the right way for the kid who sits behind you in English class. Now, your way of fitting in might be by fitting *out!* I mean, you might decide that you don't want to fit in at all and that you want to be a loner, an outsider, your own person 100 percent. Maybe you just don't want to play the social game in school or in your neighborhood. To me, that's OK. Maybe it even means that you're some kind of hero, as long as you feel right about it. Or, it could be you just want to fit in a little. I'm pretty sure that's how I am. Or, you may want to fit in sometimes but not always, or else you might want to fit in in some ways but not always in all ways (my constantly-criticizing-me English teacher would say, "Clever use of words, Jarvis, but watch those run-on sentences.") Who knows what's the best way to fit in or how you decide? It's a problem, I guess, if you don't feel right about how you fit in socially, because it can do bad things to you like make you upset too much of the time.

Before we get any further into all of this, my reading public, I have to tell you something. I know you are not reading this fascinating book to find out more about the secret private life of Jarvis Clutch, Social Spy. But I have to tell you about a nutty dream I had the other night (my teachers say I also dream during the day in their classes, making me a full-time dreamer). In this dream of mine, there were some kids who were pretty popular, and they were all together at someone's house watching a video and having pizza with everything on it and drinking lemonade with chocolate fudge sauce and mayonnaise (a drink dreams are made of). I wanted to be with them, but when I tried to get into the house, the door was locked. I tried a bunch of different keys. Some of them were bigger than I was (you know how dreams are). Other keys were made of thin glass and kept breaking in half, and one was rubber and kept bending. Another key was sizzling hot and burned my fingers. I just couldn't unlock that door between me and the kids I wanted to be with. I felt horrible; it was like a nightmare. Man, it *was* a nightmare. When I woke up, I thought about that dream for a while. I realized that social life is just like that. It's like you have a key inside you, and you have to find the lock that your social key fits. Then you can unlock your social life, the social life that is right for you. See, I'm even smarter than I seem (and talk and act). I figured out that, just like different keys fit in different locks, different kids fit with different groups of other kids or different kinds of social life. If you find where your key fits, you open the door to feeling right socially. Brilliant, isn't it, if I do say so myself.

FRIENDSHIP AND POPULARITY

I'm sure you already know that a big part of being successful socially is having friends and knowing something about *friendship* and how it's supposed to work. You know, friendship and *popularity* will come up a whole lot in this book because they kinda hang together and yet they're different, and they are both really important to social success. In my spy work, one thing that I have picked up about friendship is that a lot of boys pick friends that like to do the same things they like to do and a lot of girls pick friends they can talk to easily. A girl might say to a friend, "Hey, let's get together on Saturday." A boy would say, "Let's go ride our bikes on Saturday." Boys always seem to need an activity as an excuse for friendship. I know this guy Charlie who told me that he was really good friends with Trent because Trent has a basketball hoop in his driveway. It's the game that got them together.

But back to the difference between friendship and popularity. The totally strange thing is that there are some kids who are popular, but who don't have any real friends. There are also kids who have friends, who aren't popular. The thing is, friends are people you're really close to and you really enjoy. You can trust friends, you can tell them secrets, you can let your real feelings out with them, and you can have a good time with them. I know a girl named Hannah who weighs much too much and has social problems because of that. But you know what? I asked Hannah if she feels lonely, and she said no. Hannah explained to your Social Spy that she has a few close friends and a cousin her age who live near her, and they all spend a whole lot of time together. Well, this is what made me realize that there are two parts to social life—one is being popular and the other is having friends. You probably already knew that. You get the difference? It is possible to have some truly good friends without being popular. When you're popular, you know everyone (or at least a huge number of folks), and they all want to be with you. It's like you have a big fan club or something. That's different from having close friendships, I think. Take this kid I call Jake the Jock. He's very, very popular at Eastern Middle School. I've never heard of anybody more popular than Jake, this football hero. He's world famous in the little world of our school, which is the only world that most kids around here know about. But I have a feeling that Jake has no real friends, nobody he's close to. He knows everybody, but he doesn't know anyone well. So, reader, Jarvis is reporting to you that it is possible to have friends without being popular (like Hannah), and it is also possible to be popular without having real friends (like Jake). I have to report, of course, that there are some kids who are popular who also have friends. And then there are some who are unpopular who have no friends! Anything's possible. Let's ask Dr. Levine what he thinks about my brilliant discovery. Doc?

• DR. LEVINE COMMENTS ON FRIENDSHIP AND POPULARITY •

I think Jarvis is absolutely right—some kids have friends but are not trying to be popular with large numbers of kids. But to figure out where you fit into the social scene, from time to time, all students and probably all grownups, too, have to ask themselves a couple of big questions: How and where do I fit in socially? and What should my social life be like? In grown-up terms, someone might ask: what's your social status? In kid terms that simply means: where and how do you fit into the social scene out there? Do you feel OK about this? Is this right for you?

• • •

It is natural to want to be accepted by others. Being part of a group is one way that kids find acceptance. This diagram shows some of the reasons why students decide to fit in with a group.

WHY BEING PART OF A GROUP MAKES MANY KIDS FEEL GOOD

They feel protected.

They have people that they can trust.

They feel wanted and admired.

They feel liked.

They feel as if they have a second family.

They are with others who like doing what they like doing.

Everybody, or at least nearly everybody, wants to be wanted. In the social world, that means that we have a desire to be accepted by others. In school, that might consist of being accepted into a group of students who spend time together and enjoy being with each other. We all know how great it feels to be accepted by a group you like and respect, and how painful it can be when a group you would love to be a part of rejects you and won't let you in. So, for many people a big aspect of fitting in socially involves finding a group to which you can belong. Sometimes it is possible to belong to several groups. Then, there are some who prefer not to belong to any groups. They like to be by themselves, and this works because most of the time you can be a loner if you want to without making enemies of students who are in groups. Students who are in groups may even respect you for your independence. What this all means is that students have a lot of choices when it comes to fitting in (or fitting out).

Because groups play such a big role in the social scene at school, I asked Jarvis to do some spying on the groups at Eastern Middle School this year. I think he made some important discoveries, which he is going to tell us about now.

BELONGING TO GROUPS

This is Jarvis following orders like a good kid. I studied and studied the groups of kids that hang around together at Eastern Middle School, and the first thing I did was to interview some of my fellow unfortunate, overworked, underpaid students to find out how they feel about being part of a group of friends. Here are some things they told me:

• "Being part of a group of friends makes me feel wanted."

- "My group lets me know that there are some things about me that other kids like and admire. Without them, I might feel inferior to everyone."

- "Being with my group of friends makes me feel really warm inside; I am at my happiest when I'm with my little group of friends."

- "This may sound weird, but when I'm with the group I feel protected. It's like wearing a bulletproof vest. I'm always running a little bit scared when I'm all alone, but when I'm in my group, nothing else matters. I feel as though no one and nothing can get me. It's as if they are watching out for me. Even though I know that's not really completely true, I still feel that way. I am willing to do things with my friends that I would never dare to do alone."

- "When I'm with my group of friends, I never feel bored; there are always things to do. I am with the kids I'm with because they like to do the same things I like to do. It's always more fun than I could ever have alone or with a different group of kids. I mean, friends are fun, real fun."

- "I can trust my friends; I can tell them secrets. I need them so I can talk about how I really feel about things."

- "My group of friends is like a family. A lot of times I like them better than my real family. I get into lots of arguments with my parents and my sisters, but I can always go back to my family of friends and feel very good—and close. It's peaceful."

- "People don't realize how dangerous it is to be a kid in middle school. You're always a little scared, scared of your teachers and maybe mostly scared of other kids, of getting picked on or embarrassed or even hurt physically. But when you're in a group, it's as if you have your own private security guards protecting you. They don't really guard you, but others are less likely to go after you if you have a group on your side—or at least that's the feeling you get when you're part of a group. Life's not as scary."

Well, reader, that's all pretty powerful stuff. Being part of a group has lots of advantages. You know, grown-ups keep using the word *self-esteem*. Have you ever heard that one? When I first heard it, I thought my mom was talking about "selfish steam," which I decided was the hot air I give off when I talk too much, which I do a lot. Adults seem to love talking about self-esteem. Probably most of them have problems with it. Very brilliant guys like Levine would say that being part of a group helps your self-esteem. Knowing other kids want you around helps you feel as if you must be worth something. There's nothing like being in demand. That makes sense. I guess if you're not part of a group, you have to find some other way to build up your self-esteem. Who knows, maybe sometimes that's good for you. Your Social Spy recommends that you don't try to get every single bit of your self-esteem from belonging to a group—just some of it.

You certainly have to give your group credit for keeping you entertained, helping you feel good about yourself, protecting you, and letting you escape (or at least take a much-needed recess) from your own family hassling, criticizing, over-loving, disciplining, and bugging you, not to mention making you take your vitamins. Of course, you gotta give your parents credit, too. They're cool, even fun a lot of the time, but it's still great to have friends. They give you a different kind of fun. But you know, I have found in my spying that sometimes groups can be dangerous to your health and can even wreck your life. We have some kids who belong to gangs, and they feel terrific when they're with the gang, and they think they're the greatest show on earth because they are part of a gang. And then, whammo, they get into burning hot water because they do anything the gang wants them to do, things they never would have done without the gang. They might get into big-time trouble like even with the law or with drugs and stuff. Or they get so far behind in school that they can never catch up, so they drop out. Then, one day, the gang disappears, and they have nothing left in their lives. My mom says that this happens a lot, and I wish I could warn those kids while they're in middle school. But I know that they wouldn't listen.

There are lots of good groups that you can belong to. You can have a small bunch of friends, or you can join a club, a team, or a thing grown-ups like to run (like Scouts or some kind of church group). Also, I think you can be completely part of a group or partly part of a group, if you know what I mean. The group can suck you in totally, all the time, or you can be with the group some of the time for some things, and maybe even with a different group part of the time for some other things. There are hundreds of possibilities. It looks as if you have to find out what works for you. I'm still trying to figure this out. But that's what middle school is for, at least partly some of the time.

I have found that at Eastern Middle School we are most definitely clumped into groups. We are a divided nation. And you know when I see this the most? During lunch. I can pretty much tell you which kids are going to sit together. Now, obviously, there are groups of kids that can't eat together because they do not have the same lunch hour (a brilliant Jarvis discovery). But you see them after school or marching through the mall on Saturday or making a big clump somewhere else. But here are some groups that have their lunch meetings every single day. There's a table with nothing but jocks—mostly boys. They talk sports all the time. There's a group of mostly girls I call "the preps" because they look as if they have lots of money, and they wear expensive clothes (which they talk about all the time). There's a table that just has mostly black kids eating at it, but sometimes one or two white students join them, and nobody seems to mind. There are five or six Chinese (I think they're Chinese) boys and girls that eat together and sometimes talk in their language, but they don't use chopsticks or anything like that to eat their fish sticks. Then there's a group that talks half Spanish and half English. One table of girls has been together as long as I can remember; their specialty seems to be gossiping and babbling without having to breathe. I'm not sure how they all got together, but it's as if they've been welded with some kind of a talking soldering iron. Then there is a table of mostly guys who I think are much more interested in astronomy and math and computers and science fiction than they are in each other. But they hang together— loosely. Each one mainly does his own thing. There's also a tight group that all wear all black all the time; you gotta feel a little scared of them because some of them look to me like troublemakers who could be out to get you if you don't watch out, unless of course you're lucky or unlucky enough to become one of them. They don't attack their own members—at least not usually. Last but not least, we have the geeks, who are so uncool that I think they're cool! We all know who they are. There are plenty of other groups, but these are the easiest ones for your Social Spy to spot from a distance.

Now, don't get me wrong, not every group at Eastern Middle School contains kids who are exactly the same; some of them have different kinds of kids who happen to like each other. I mean, there are some "mix" groups with a few jocks and some preps, and even one or two other species of middle school wildlife. But you know what I have discovered? The more they hang around together, the more they become more and more like each other. Is that good or bad? Who knows? But it scares me a little that if I got into some group and spent all my time with them, I might stop being the real Jarvis, the person I love and admire so much—just kidding.

There are also some kids who eat all by themselves. They look just a little tiny bit embarrassed about that. It makes me sad to see them sitting alone. It feels as if this is their first day in a new school and they don't know anybody. But they've been around since kindergarten. It's really hard to tell if they want to be loners or if they have real trouble making friends. Who knows? Maybe some people want to be by themselves, even though they don't have to be. But some of them have to be alone because no one seems to want to be with them.

Spying on all these groups has made me wonder how kids decide which group to be in. Does it just happen by accident? I mean, you don't usually fill out an application and pay some money to get in with a group of friends. I think most kids seem to want to be with kids who are most like them. Sometimes I wonder why it wouldn't be more fun for them to hang around with people who are totally different from them. I guess that's human nature or something. It looks to me as if close friends seem to come from the same kind of background or even ethnic group, or else they like to do the same kind of stuff (like play basketball or video games, or collect hubcaps). I also wonder how often kids get kicked out of a group and why that happens. Life is never easy for us middle school sufferers, is it, Levine?

• DR. LEVINE COMMENTS ON SOCIAL PRESSURE •

Jarvis is right on target when he says that life is not easy for most middle schoolers. The social part of their lives can be especially confusing and stressful. When this part is working well, it is where kids have the most fun and get to feel really good about themselves, but when it's not going well, this part can be the most trying part of life. Recently, I met with a group of middle school students at their school. I asked them which was harder for them, social pressure or academic pressure. Every single one of them said that social pressure was rougher! Everyone's social life has its ups and downs. As we have seen in this chapter, fitting in is important to many students, and it often involves being part of one, two, or maybe even several groups of kids who seem to like you and want to include you in what they do. Of course, there are some people who might only want to fit in with one or two close friends and not with a whole group. Life gets rough when you can't get accepted by the group or even the person you would like to be with. Sometimes this happens when kids have weaknesses in their social cognition so they don't seem right, talk right, or act right with others.

PEER PRESSURE AND CONFORMITY

But there's another part of getting into a group and staying in it. I'm talking about *peer pressure,* which has to do with the very powerful influence that kids have over each other. Peer pressure is the pressure to seem, talk, and act a certain way, a way that fits with what others expect from you. Sometimes kids put this kind of pressure on each other on purpose, and sometimes it just happens. But what if you don't happen to agree with or like what others want you to be? Then what are you supposed to do? Do you go with the flow and conform in order to have friends, or do you insist on being yourself, even if that means you could get rejected? It's a tough decision and one that most people face sooner or later in their lives. There is

All kids have to think about how much they want to conform and be like everyone else they know and how much they would like to be their own person, even though that may make them different from other kids in important ways. The trick is to find the right balance between fitting in and being yourself.

THE BALANCE BETWEEN TRYING TO BE DIFFERENT AND TRYING TO BE LIKE EVERYBODY ELSE

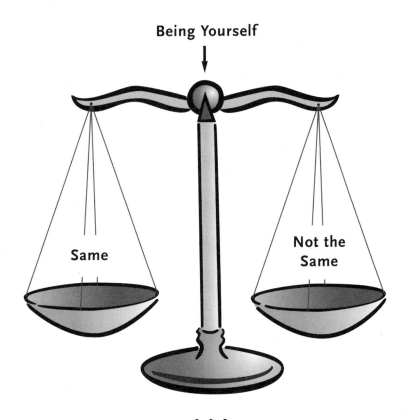

tremendous pressure to conform and to be like everybody else in your group, so that your group will accept you. The trick is to be somewhere in the middle—to try to seem right, talk right, and act right without giving up all of your freedom and becoming someone you're not, a phony or fake kid. That's not easy. Let's see what Jarvis has learned about peer pressure and conformity.

PEER PRESSURE AND CONFORMITY

Dr. Levine, I have spied on a lot of kids that I would call total, complete, 100 percent pure conformists. They sort of remind me of chameleons, because they change their color to fit in with their surroundings. Take this kid named Manuel. He's as smooth as whipped cream. He dresses just right and looks as if he could be a model for someone who sells face transplants. He uses all the right "in" words when he talks, and he likes exactly the same music that most of the coolest kids at Eastern Middle School listen to. It's like he lives in a country with a dictator, and the dictator is all the other kids. He says and does whatever most everyone else says and does. In my opinion, Manuel is a social wimp-servant—he has no freedom to be himself. He doesn't know who he really is. He's only what other people force him to be. I don't like that at all. But you know what, reader? Manuel seems like a really happy kid. He has plenty of friends and he has loads of fun. Other kids really like him, and he is accepted in several different groups. This kid just plain fits in, for sure. He may be Eastern Middle School's most socially fit fitter-in. Fitting in that well would give me a fit. (English teacher, please note my very clever wordplay. "Thank you, Jarvis Clutch.") But I wouldn't want to be like Manuel the fitter-in. I don't really know; maybe I couldn't be like him even if I wanted to be. Peer pressure confuses me—and a lot of other people, too, I bet.

BEING DIFFERENT ENOUGH AND BEING YOURSELF

Then there are kids at Eastern Middle School who are just exactly the opposite of Manuel. They want to be different. Maybe they *have* to be different. It could be that they have no choice. I mean, they just don't fit in with everyone else.

They want to dress a certain way that's not cool. Or maybe they like to listen to Beethoven or stuff like that. Or else, maybe they really enjoy doing things that are different from what most others like. There's one kid named Reed, who takes ballet lessons, and they say he's an amazing dancer for his age. Well, that really seems to drive certain students nuts; they just won't let Reed be himself and do his thing. He danced at our holiday assembly (it was something about a nutcracker), and I decided to spy on the kids sitting in my row in the auditorium. You should have heard the giggling when poor Reed came out wearing those tights and whirling around with all those dancing girls. You could see where his private parts were! Later on, kids made fun of him; they called him a fag. And you know what? The fact that he dances around on a stage doesn't mean that he's gay or something. That doesn't make sense. Besides, if Reed is gay, who cares? That's just the way he's meant to be, I guess. Everybody's got a right to be himself or herself. Even though other kids tease him, Reed keeps on dancing because he really likes it, and he's good at it and probably getting better all the time. Reed wants to be different. He is fighting battles against peer pressure all the time so that he can do his thing. Being different is not easy at Eastern Middle School; I know that because I'm pretty different myself. I think it's important to be yourself. But maybe it's not always so simple to know who you are. Sometimes I feel like shouting really loud, "Hey kids, this is the real Jarvis whether you like it or not. What you see is what you get. Take it or leave it, you guys." But you know, reader, that's not so easy.

Now here's another twist for you: some kids start out like Reed and fit in absolutely nowhere and with no one except in their own little world (like a dancing stage), but then out of the blue, an amazing thing takes place. Yes, reader, they get discovered. Other people find their strengths. You see, that's what happened with this girl Lateisha, but in her case her explosion into the world of middle school raving popularity maybe wasn't so good for her. Lateisha was never popular at all in elementary school. She was mostly by herself from what I could tell. But she was some kind of genius student, at the top of her class in all subjects. She read a lot and was a whiz in math. Then something snapped. She got to be about thirteen years old. That's when this kid drowned in her own hormones. Lateisha, just like out of nowhere, picked up really good looks and some very visible body changes. I mean, her body grew up super fast in all the right ways. All of a sudden guys got interested in Lateisha for the first time, and the other girls started to include Lateisha in everything they did. At home, the phone kept ringing for Lateisha with heaps of invitations. It was like a fierce tornado of popularity. I have spied on Lateisha, and she is a prized possession of her friends. But guess what? Lateisha is now failing English and math. She has stopped studying and handing in her homework. I bet her parents are totally freaked out by this change. My mom says Lateisha won't even talk to her own mom anymore, except maybe to fight and argue about her freedom. She's got no interest in her family. She only cares about her friends. You can be sure that Lateisha feels so great about her sudden popularity that nothing else matters to her anymore. It's as if she got rich quick. If she had been popular all along when she was younger, she wouldn't have gotten such a high from being popular in middle school. Now schoolwork can't compete with her friends. But you have to wonder what will happen to her when all of her loving followers suddenly disappear after high school. What will Lateisha be left with? She's paying a fortune for fitting in. But that's just my opinion. I mean, we do have some kids at Eastern who are popular *and* they do well in school. It can be done. It's done all the time. I hope it's not too late for Lateisha.

THE OPPOSITE SEX (FROM YOU!)

Boys and girls hang together a lot at Eastern Middle School. What I have noticed in my spying is that there are two kinds of hanging around together. There's the sort where it really doesn't matter who's a girl and who's a boy; they're all just friends. Then there's the kind of hanging around where they're thinking about going on dates or having a girlfriend or boyfriend. Then who's a boy and who's a girl becomes a real thing. That's different from just plain hanging out together. This dating thing is rough.

To keep things pretty simple, I have not done much spying to try to figure out how to act with the opposite sex—what guys should do to get along with girls and what girls should do to be friends with boys. I get a little embarrassed with that stuff. Probably these things take a whole lot of social cognition to pull off. Dr. Levine would tell us that the same old abilities you use to seem right, talk right, and act right get tried out when you go out on dates or just hang around with kids of the opposite sex. I can tell you that at Eastern Middle School, it is considered ultra-cool to have a boyfriend or a girlfriend and to get invited to boy-girl parties. It is also very desirable to get talked about (in a good way) by people you would want to have as a boyfriend or girlfriend. But I can honestly tell you that the whole thing is very confusing, at least to me, Jarvis, the Social Spy.

As I cruise the corridors, classrooms, and ugly offices at Eastern, it's kind of mind-boggling. Some kids act as if they are ready to get married by the middle of seventh grade. They claim to be very into sex and stuff—maybe they are, I don't know. Others keep getting divorces. I mean, they have these fierce romances and then BOOM! The shot heard 'round the world! You find out they're breaking up. Of course, I couldn't care less, but some kids thrive on the gossip. A lot of Eastern Middle Schoolers don't have any interest in the opposite sex or in any sex. They still want to do kid things. Others are very shy, and they act as if they are afraid to get near someone of the opposite sex—unless it's inside a classroom, where it's all business. Then there are some kids who don't really care about the opposite sex, but they make believe that they do—just to impress everyone else. That doesn't work on your favorite Social Spy. I can see right through all their fakery with my social X-ray vision. It's as if their skulls were made out of glass.

Well, I guess all this adds up to one huge idea: there are a lot of different ways to be normal in middle school. All this sex stuff and how it fits with your personal life and your social life depends on what suits you, if you ask me, and there are plenty of differences among kids. Everyone has a right to be different—as long as it's not harmful to them or anyone else. Do you agree, Dr. L.?

• THE MANY WAYS TO BE NORMAL •

Yes, Jarvis, it's amazing how many ways there are to be a normal person. That means that kids need to figure out how to be themselves and feel good about being themselves. At the same time, of course, they have to figure out how to fit in with others, or decide if they'd rather not fit in at all. Some kids really have a true desire to have a boyfriend or girlfriend and some don't.

Both kinds of kids are normal. But then there are some students who have or try to have girlfriends and boyfriends because they think it looks cool or they believe they can't really be popular without proving they can attract someone special. I suppose they're mainly showing off.

. . .

Kids often experiment with or try out different ways of fitting in. Everyone does it—at least once in a while. But as you can see in the diagram, some of these experiments are safe and others may have too high a price to pay for fitting in. Those bad experiments can even shorten your life!

Pretty Safe Experiments

Social Experiments Designed to Impress Other Kids

Dangerous Experiments

Changing Appearance

Developing New Interests

Trying New Tastes in Things

Smoking/Drugs

Losing Too Much Weight

Breaking the Law

All of this brings up another important issue, and that is the way many kids experiment with acting like an adult. They try on adulthood the way they might try on an article of clothing in a store. That, too, is normal. Likewise, some kids may date because they feel it will make them seem more mature; that's usually an experiment. Very often students who smoke got started because they wanted to look older, more adult. Of course, then they can't stop smoking and they are subjecting their bodies to getting cancer or heart disease someday—just because they wanted to look older faster! That's quite a price to pay for experimenting with adulthood. Of course, some of these experiments also include using drugs or maybe overdoing sexual activity.

You may be wondering what the connection is between fitting in and social cognition. It's really quite simple: it takes social cognition to decide how you should fit in and then to fit in the way you'd like to fit in. Kids with social cognition weaknesses may have trouble figuring out how they should fit in. Then, as if to make their lives even rougher, they can have difficulties seeming right, talking right, and acting right in ways that are needed to fit in in the way they want to fit in! Some kids feel unhappy deep down in their hearts because they are not fitting in right. They may come to envy kids that are accepted. It can be very depressing to learn that other kids are being invited to do things and no one ever calls you or wants to do things with you. You feel rejected and neglected.

SOCIAL PREDATORS AND BULLYING

And sometimes life gets really scary when, in addition to not fitting in, you are a victim of *bullying*. Other kids may pick on you, threaten you, make fun of you, or even push you around or hurt you physically. We call the kids who do this *social predators*. A *predator* is an animal that preys on other animals and tries to hurt or kill them. Believe it or not, there are some kids who act like predators. I believe that Jarvis has spied on them and can let us in on what he has found out.

JARVIS ON SOCIAL PREDATORS AND BULLYING

Yes, Dr. Levine, I can. I have spied on Eastern Middle School's vicious and sleazy social predators, and I have made some startling discoveries. First of all, let me tell you about two kids named Zach and Molly. Zach and Molly are very popular. They try to be beautiful people, and a lot of kids look up to them and want to be with them and maybe would even like to *be* them. Yes, they are respected (and feared) leaders of what our principal Mr. Maloney (sometimes lovingly known as Phony Baloney Maloney) calls "our wonderful Eastern Middle School family." (Sometimes our "wonderful" family is called "marvelous" when he gets tired of calling it "wonderful.") Anyway, there is this poor kid named Simon, who is very short for his age, and is really bad at sports, plus he says weird things, plays chess, and loves raising saltwater fish. Simon's voice kinda squeaks as if he needs to swallow a can of oil, and he wears really thick glasses with scratched up, dirty-looking plastic rims that sometimes have a piece of tape around them. To tell the truth, according to how Eastern Middle School students think about each other, Simon is the opposite of what they mean when they use the word *cool*! Too bad. I think he's a nice guy. Simon's smart, interesting, honest, and always kind to every-one. But he has no social cognition in him—not one ounce of the things we'll talk about later in this book that are needed to be popular. He has one or two not-very-close-friends (including Jarvis the Social Spy), but that's about it. Man, does he get picked on, and reader, guess who leads the attack? Yep, our hero and heroine, Zach and Molly. Zach calls him Slimy Simon and con-stantly does things to embarrass him—especially in front of Zach's adoring crowds. Like the other day he tripped Simon and tossed his binder on the wet ground. The binder came apart, and a lot of Simon's papers got mud all over them. The Molly and Zach fan club thought this was the most hilarious sight they had ever seen. Poor Simon, you could tell he wanted to cry, but he was afraid to. He felt so bad, so worthless, and so helpless. He didn't know what to do. So he crawled along the ground picking up his papers while Zach called him more names and everybody laughed. Then somebody intentionally stepped on Simon's left hand—which hurt a lot, but he still didn't cry. At thirteen, he thought he was too old to cry.

A couple of weeks ago, Zach grabbed Simon's glasses in the locker room, and he hid them in a locker. The thing is, Simon needs his glasses to see. He went stumbling and fumbling around in his purple striped boxer shorts with a small hole over the right rear (which is much better than a hole in the front, in my opinion) looking for them. Zach tried to pull down Simon's shorts, but he didn't manage to do it. Simon was so scared. What Zach did to Simon was considered fantastic humor by a lot of the other boys. They seemed to respect him for being able to put down a pretty helpless person. Soon, they all left to go to their classes. Simon was alone in the locker room, except for me. I helped him find his glasses and I let him know how cruel and stupid I thought those kids were, but Simon didn't seem to want to talk about it. Simon and I both got detention for being late for Spanish class. We were afraid to tell the teacher what had happened because if Zach got in trouble he could turn on both of us and make even more trouble. Simon thought about telling his parents what was going on in school, but he was afraid they would call Mr. Maloney, and Zach would then get a lecture from our principal, and that would make him go completely ballistic—then there would be big, big trouble for poor Simon. Later, Zach and his crowd told a bunch of girls that they should take up a collection to buy Simon new boxers to replace his dirty, torn ones, and Simon explained to me that he had had his feelings hurt so many times and had been completely embarrassed so often that it didn't matter to him. He also said that he was used to feeling depressed. I wanted to help Simon feel good, so I said (and meant it), "Simon, you are so smart and you have so much more ability than Zach. I bet he'll be working for you someday." Simon smiled.

Don't be surprised to learn that Molly can be just as vicious as her boy-eating boyfriend. But her methods are a little different. Molly's secret weapon is gossip. She spreads rumors about kids she doesn't like or maybe about kids she's afraid don't like her. And she makes sure that the students she's targeted don't get invited to any important parties. For example, there's this girl at Eastern named Noriko who loves horses and dresses as if her favorite stallion slept on her clothes. Molly told all her friends that Noriko wishes she were a boy (not true, by the way, according to my interview with Noriko). She also spread the word that Noriko's parents beat her all the time (not true) and that Noriko is always trying to kill herself (also untrue). Once Noriko invited some girls to go horseback riding at a stable thirty or forty miles away. Her parents were willing to drive everyone there, since it was Noriko's birthday. Molly told the girls who were invited that she would never speak to them again if they went to that horse party. And you know what? Noriko had to ride by herself on her birthday. She didn't invite me; I think I would have accepted. But I don't care what Molly thinks. Lots of other kids do, though.

Some of the social predators at Eastern act like they're earning their living by making fun of other students, usually for things those students can't help.

Take me, for example. I have a name that is not considered to be a truly cool name. Could you ever imagine someone with a name like Jarvis Clutch being the most popular kid in his class? No way. Man, my popularity ratings dropped way down when I was less than a day old, the first time my name got mentioned in public! There are now times when some of the more vicious citizens of Eastern Middle School put me down in public just because of the name I didn't pick for myself. Yup, you got it; I get called Jarvis Klutz, especially in P.E. class. A whole bunch of kids laugh when I get called that. I never know how I'm supposed to react. I try to ignore it, but it hurts, at least a little bit, every single time. I keep wanting to shout, "You guys, I didn't wake up one morning and decide to be called Jarvis Clutch instead of Jim Smith! Cool it! It's not my fault!"

Yes, reader, it is sad but true that some of our most popular students seem to try to increase their power and their popularity by leading the attack on kids who are different from them or don't have the right kind of social cognition to get in with them. I have to say, it's not always true that the most popular students do this kind of thing, but it seems to be pretty common around here at the world's most wonderful middle school.

EXPERIMENTING WITH FITTING IN

Here's what I've decided after all these months of spying on other kids: a whole lot of what they do (and maybe some of what I do) are really social life experiments, like the ones we do in science class, but you don't have to write these up. I think kids keep experimenting on each other and experimenting on themselves too. Hair experiments are big-time at our school.

Eastern girls experiment with different ways to tangle or mess up or glue up their hair. Some of them keep dyeing or cutting their hair. The boys are also into hair science. It seems as if each time they do something hairy with their hair, they are experimenting with becoming a new person. It's almost like Halloween all year round. Everybody keeps trying out different disguises. They're like a test model of a new car.

In my spy work, I came across this girl, Suzanne, who tries to change into a completely new person at least every two weeks—you know, with a new hair color (last week it was purple), different stuff smeared on her face, or some new, exciting hunk of hardware screwed into her skin somewhere. It's as if she's trying to figure out what works for her, what will make her fit into the Eastern scene just the way she wants to. Other kids experiment by smoking or drinking or using drugs. And there are some who keep experimenting to find out how it feels and looks to be a grown-up. They do lots of things to seem like adults, including some of the smoking and dressing that they think makes them look nineteen instead of thirteen. You know, I personally think it's a little weird that kids want to experiment with being grown-up when, all around this town, I see plenty of grown-ups who are trying to experiment with looking younger than they are. Why can't people just be the age they are? A lot of times it's unpleasant, but I don't mind being fourteen too much. I think I'll wait till I'm nineteen to be nineteen. I have enough problems without having all that experimenting to think about!

By the way, I need to let you know that there are some students here at Eastern who want to experiment, and they do, but they do a terrible job of experimenting and so they look or act totally ridiculous a lot of the time. I guess it takes some social cognition to do good social experiments. There's this kid named Virgil who does nothing but very bad experiments that backfire on him. To make friends the other day, he started giving out disgusting peanut brittle that he had baked at home the night before. He thought that would make kids think he was generous and a nice guy. They didn't. One day he came to school with all of his hair shaved off, thinking that would be considered extra cool. Nobody cared. Then he brought in pictures of his dad's new pickup truck and showed them to the kids sitting near him at lunch. Forget it! He didn't have the social cognition to do experiments that might have a chance of working. Poor guy.

Here's another even more tragic tale of social experimenting gone wrong. It's about a friend of my big brother, Jeremy. You should know that I'm not Jeremy's biggest fan. Anyway, this kid named Andrew is a lot like my brother. He's a good athlete, a super student, good looking, popular and all that. But Andrew liked being liked so much that he kept trying to do things to get liked even more by other kids. It was as if he was hooked on friends. One night about six months ago, my brother, Andrew, and Andrew's girlfriend, Ana, all went to a big party. You have to understand that Andrew usually did everything the way a kid his age is supposed to do things; he never stepped out of line. But somehow, this night he decided to get drunk, just as an experiment. He thought it would be cool; everyone would talk about it at school the next week. Besides, he had been under a whole lot of pressure in school and felt kind of stressed out. So he drank loads of beer. Then he drove home with Ana. They got into a very bad accident, a really serious one. Andrew's mother's car got totaled, and Ana broke her arm. Andrew got seriously hurt. He's now in a wheelchair and will never walk again because his spine got cut in half. That's a true story. Andrew paid a huge price for his experiment in super coolness. Things like that happen all the time.

Dr. Levine has informed me that he has one final aspect of fitting in to tell us all about. So I will now let him have his book space. (I have to show him respect because he's older than I am—by a lot.) Actually, Dr. Levine is going to say a few words about what he calls the politics of being a kid. To tell you the truth, I have no idea what that's all about.

• POLITICS AND POLITICAL SKILL •

Whenever you read the newspaper or watch a news program on TV, you hear about politics. But what do we mean by politics? *Politics* are the methods or tactics people use to have positive relationships with people who are important to them (whether they like them or not). So when a politician is running for mayor or governor and tries very hard to win over as many voters as he or she can in order to win an election, that's politics. Or when people are very nice to their boss so that they can get a higher salary, that's politics, too. Or when people try to be nice to all their neighbors because they want them to stop complaining about their dog barking, that, too, is politics.

Kids may not realize it, but their lives are also very political. Being good politically is one more important way of fitting in. Some kids have much better political skills than others. Your political skills are part of your social cognition, having to do with how well you interact with people who could be important to you and to your future. Probably the best example of this is how positively you relate to your teachers. After all, your teachers give you grades on stories you write, quizzes, and report cards. They may even write comments about you. Grades and comments can affect your ability to get a job or get into the college you'd like to go to. If a teacher is trying to decide whether to give you a *B* or a *C* in a course, and that teacher likes you very much, you have a better chance of getting the *B*. However, if that teacher has negative feelings toward you, the *C* has an excellent chance of showing up on your report card. After all, teachers are only human. But whether or not a teacher likes you may depend at least partly on how good a politician you are. Do you show an interest in class? Looking bored all the time is not good politics. Do you say anything to make your teachers feel good about themselves (and therefore about you, too)? This can be politically important—as long as it's not totally artificial. (Kids call this political tactic *brown-nosing* or *kissing up*.) Do you behave right and participate actively in class or do you sit there looking as if you are above all this math junk? Acting as if you are too cool or smart to care about schoolwork is politically stupid—it really bugs your teachers. Also, students need to realize that teachers in middle school and high school have lots of students, but students have just a few teachers. That means that it's the student who has to form good relationships with teachers—not the other way around. That can be hard for kids with weak political skills.

You even need some political skill to relate to student leaders in your school. You don't want to get on their bad side, even if you don't care to be friends with them. Elections to student government provide another example of politics. You have to know how to sell yourself to other kids if you want to be president of your class, head of the chess club, or captain of the girls' basketball team.

I think kids get some of their first lessons in politics when they try to get along with their brothers or sisters. There's always competition in a family. Each kid wants some attention, freedom, and power. Then there are kids who don't have any brothers or sisters. Only children don't get as much political experience at home, and learning how politics works at school can be harder for them because they don't have as much practice. No matter how many (if any!) brothers and sisters kids have, all kids who understand the politics of their family get some valuable lessons. Politically smart kids know how to make their parents feel that they are good parents. Mothers and fathers can love their children very much without really liking them. It takes some political skill to have parents who love you and also like you. That means that your parents like to be with you, talk to you, and boast about you. You should think about how kids get their parents to like them. The politics of each family are different.

Does the idea of politics make more sense to you now, Jarvis?

JARVIS ON POLITICS

Yes, Dr. Levine. I even have a couple of short political tales to tell. In my classes at Eastern Middle School, I have spied on kids to see how they try to get along with their teachers and classmates, and I can tell you that there are some very big differences.

There's this one kid, Andre, who acts really gross in class. I am sure that almost all his teachers can't stand the guy or his brain. I mean, Andre is pretty smart and all that. But he argues with his teachers all the time. He acts as if he already knows everything and doesn't need to be going to school at all. He loves to disagree with things the teacher just said. The other day in social studies class, Ms. Hallowell talked about how in a democracy, everyone can vote. Andre started arguing that in a lot of places that are democracies, people are prevented from voting or they have trouble getting to the polls, so they're not really democratic countries. He included the United States in this.

The teacher tried to say that no democracy is perfect; nothing ever works perfectly. But Andre went on and on, arguing with Ms. Hallowell while she and the rest of the class got really ticked off at him.

There's no way Ms. Hallowell could feel good about Andre, even though he is intelligent and knows a lot of stuff. I mean, he had a good point and all, but he just presented it in completely the wrong way. In math, he acts bored a lot of time and argues with the teacher when he gets a bad grade. In Spanish, he sits in the back of the room and tries to be a Mr. Cool who doesn't care about anything and is willing to get into trouble. If I were Mr. Lopez, I would hate Andre and write horrible, nasty comments on his report card. Andre may be smart about some things (like facts in books), but he is a very dumb politician. Not only does he lose the votes of his teachers, but all the other kids think he acts like a jerk in class. He'd better not try to run for class president or even volunteer to head the clean-up committee at our upcoming fun-free holiday party.

Here's one more political threat: how do we handle kids who are leaders and have a lot of influence over what kids think about other kids? You sure don't want to get on the wrong side of these powerful students. But what if you don't like them? There's one really nice girl I met named Lin. She does her own thing but gets along with kids when she needs or wants to. I told Lin about my spy work at Eastern Middle School and asked if I could ask her a few things. I wanted to know what she thought about Zach and Molly—you remember these two very popular and influential eighth graders. Lin told me that she doesn't approve of the way they control so many other kids. But Lin told me about a few things she does that I think are very good politically. First, she stays out of Zach and Molly's way. She tries not to join in with their activities and circle of friends. Second, she is always nice to them—without joining their army. Third, she is quiet when she is around them. Fourth, she is careful not to say bad things about them behind their backs (except, of course, to this Social Spy). Her methods are working. Lin can be herself and have her freedom without having to worry about getting wiped out by Zach and Molly. Good work, Lin. You get an *A* in middle school politics.

Now, readers, the time has come for Dr. Levine to wrap up Chapter 2 of our book. In Chapter 3 we will continue talking about, wondering about, and arguing about this bunch of abilities called social cognition.

• DR. LEVINE ON SETTING SOCIAL GOALS •

We have had a chance to cover many important issues that come up when a kid tries to fit in. As you might have noticed, different people have different *social goals*. Some want to fit in with everyone, and others want to fit in with only one person or one group or a few groups of people. Then there are always individuals who choose not to fit in at all. That's OK unless the only reason they choose not to fit in is that they really don't know how to fit in (deep down in their hearts they may really want to). Often, these are kids with weak social cognition.

GETTING HELP WITH SOCIAL COGNITION AND FITTING IN

We all have to decide how to fit in with other people. Then we can go about trying to live lives that work well for us socially, whether our social cognition is weak or strong. For the kids who have weaknesses in social cognition, this may be difficult. They may not be able to seem right, talk right, or act right to others. For them, fitting in may be very hard or almost impossible. On the other hand, some kids find taking charge of their social life very easy; they don't even think about it. They have plenty of friends and they have a great time when they're with them.

For kids whose social lives aren't working out the way they'd like, there are different ways that they can get help. Sometimes their parents can review social issues and help them figure out how to fit in in a way that's right for them. Even reading this book can be helpful, especially if it makes kids review their own social cognition and decide which areas need improvement. Some students go through social skills training programs that are available in some schools or communities. Others get help with their social cognition from a counselor or teacher. But I think all kids can benefit from thinking about their social lives—whether or not they seem successful.

In the box below you will find a summary of the issues involved in fitting in:

HAVING FRIENDS AND/OR BEING POPULAR

BELONGING TO A GROUP

HANDLING PEER PRESSURE AND CONFORMITY

TRYING TO BE DIFFERENT AND BEING YOURSELF

RELATING TO THE OPPOSITE SEX

DEALING WITH SOCIAL PREDATORS

EXPERIMENTING WITH YOUR SOCIAL LIFE

BECOMING POLITICALLY SKILLED

SETTING SOCIAL GOALS

GETTING HELP WITH SOCIAL COGNITION

1. What is meant by *fitting in and feeling good about it?* Is it possible to feel good about *not* fitting in? How would you react if a student said to you, "I don't really care if I fit in with anyone or not. I just want to be myself and do what I want to do"?

2. Do you think there are big differences between the ways boys relate to other boys and the ways girls relate to other girls? If so, what are these differences?

3. Do you think it is possible to be popular without having any real friends? How does that occur? Do you think it is possible to have some good friends but not be popular? Is that a good way to be?

4. Is it easy to have plenty of friends without being part of a group?

5. What would make you want to be part of a group of students?

6. Is it possible to be part of a group without acting pretty much like everyone else in the group?

7. Are you part of a group? How are you similar and in what ways are you different from other members of your group? If someone were to give your group a name, what do you think it would be called?

8. Are there groups of kids who usually eat lunch together in your school? What kinds of things do the kids who eat lunch together have in common?

9. What is meant by the term *peer pressure?* Do you think there's a lot of it in your school? Give some examples of when you have felt peer pressure.

10. What are some ways to resist peer pressure without "turning off" other kids?

11. What is conformity? Do you think kids are under a lot of pressure to conform, to seem like most others in their school? How can someone resist conformity and still have a good reputation? Is that easy or hard to do in your school?

12. How important is it to have a boyfriend or girlfriend in your school? Does it help you be more accepted and popular if you have such a relationship?

13. Do you think a lot of teenagers want to act and look like grown-ups? If so, how and why do they do it?

14. Why do you think students start smoking? How do you feel about smoking?

15. Why do some kids pick on or bully others? Do some students feel that other kids respect them because they are so good at bullying or making fun of others?

16. What are some political actions a student takes to develop a strong relationship with teachers? Do you think some kids overdo this kind of politics?

17. Do you agree with Jarvis that you also have to be politically careful with certain "powerful" students in your school? Can you think of any examples of this?

18. What are the qualities you look for when you pick out a friend?

19. The list on the next page contains some reasons why you might be friends with someone of your same sex. Please rate each of them for how important they would be to you and then compare your answers to those of others in your class. Are there differences between the answers given by boys in your class and girls in your class?

No.	Characteristics of a Potential Friend
	He/she likes the same things I do
	He/she is good looking
	He/she is cool
	He/she lives near me
	He/she dresses like me
	He/she is a good athlete
	He/she is smart
	He/she is on a team or in a club with me
	He/she is of the same race and/or religious background as me
	He/she is someone I can confide in (share feelings and tell secrets)
	He/she is part of a group that I like being with
	He/she is someone I can play games or sports with
	He/she is interested in the same things I am
	He/she is very much like me
	He/she is completely different from me
	He/she is from a family that is not richer or poorer than mine
	He/she is unusual, different from most kids I know
	Other:
	Other:
	Other:

★ JARVIS PROJECTS FOR CHAPTER 2 ★

Writing Project 1: Make believe there's a student who gets picked on, pushed around, and made fun of at school, partly because she or he's got some trouble with social cognition and doesn't quite fit in with others. One day, another student threatens to spread rumors or physically hurt this kid, who is afraid to tell his or her parents because they'll tell the principal, who will then call the bully in, and then the bully will then make even more trouble. Make believe you are writing an anonymous e-mail to the student who is getting bullied providing some good advice about the situation and how to deal with the bullying in the future.

Writing Project 2: Make believe for some dumb reason that you are putting together a new social group of middle school students. Let's say that kids have to fill out an application to get in your super-special, big-time group. Design the application for being accepted into the group. Think of around ten questions that you would ask a kid you are thinking about having in your wonderful group. Write up the questions, and then think about what the application would look like. Be creative! Use the computer or art supplies to make up the application.

Spy Mission 1: Take out your atomic spyglasses, and check out the room (or tomb) where you eat lunch at school. Figure out how many groups you can see: which ones look popular, which ones are just kinda likable, which ones are controversial, which ones everyone neglects, and which ones are rejected. Write down the ways you could tell which kids were in each group. In what ways are group members exactly like each other, and how some kids are different but still in the group? If you are lucky or unlucky enough to be in a group, do this with your own group, too.

Spy Mission 2: Here's another thrilling adventure. Try spending a long time all by yourself (like eating alone in the lunchroom or at a restaurant). Write down how you feel, especially whether or not you feel lonely or embarrassed by being alone. Also, mention any good things you feel about being by yourself.

~ CHAPTER 3 ~
SEEMING RIGHT

It's Jarvis again—all ready to blast off on his impossible mission to discover and uncover the deepest, darkest secrets of social superstardom and social horror, and all ready to teach you how to mess up every one of your relationships with other people, if that's what you feel like doing. You will be amazed to find out how easy it can be to wreck your whole reputation without even trying! But don't touch your handheld book zapper, because you will also learn how to make friends and be liked by whoever you want to be liked by. So stand by, reader, and read on while your writer writes on—until his hand and his head get too tired to move a pencil and think (which, you will be glad to know, happens very soon).

In the last chapter (remember that one?), we carried on about fitting in and feeling good about it. Well, one of the things that helps you fit in is coming across well to others. Dr. Levine seems to have decided that there are three parts to this: seeming right, talking right, and acting right. So, this chapter is about seeming right and the next two are about talking right and acting right. I am sure that Dr. Levine will tell us that some kids are very good at these things whenever they want to be or need to be, but other kids can't quite seem right, talk right, or act right, even when they would like to. I've been doing a whole lot of thinking (which is something I usually try hard *not* to do), and I have to agree that there are times when it's important to seem right. Now, what does Jarvis, Eastern Middle School's leading so-called Social Spy, mean by *seeming right?* Actually, I'm not positive, but maybe Levine will help me out on this later in this chapter, since seeming right was basically his idea. But for now it seems that seeming seems important. Seeming seems to be how you come across to others, but it's more than how you act and talk. It's also how you look, what you enjoy, what kinds of stuff you do, what you're good at, how cool you are (whatever that means), who you hang around with, and a bunch of other little things that form almost a kind of picture of who you are or, at least, who it *seems* as if you are, which seems to be important to people who seem to be all around you almost all the time. And you'll find out (if you don't lose this book on the way home from school, which is what I've been known to do) that some kids really are what they seem to be and others try to seem to be what they don't seem to me to be or just aren't. Are you impressed? Are you confused? Please don't think I completely understand what I just wrote, reader. I'm going to reread it, and you should too.

Now go ahead and plug in your social earphones because here is something major that Jarvis has just found out. It all has to do with *evaluation*. You evaluate somebody to see how much they know or what they can do. Teachers evaluate us innocent, helpless, suffering, beaten-down students all the time when they give tests or quizzes. They check us out to see what we know. In my case they get to see how much I don't know! When I get evaluated, it's always pretty much the same: "Your son Jarvis seems so bright, but he never lives up to his potential. He is a real underachiever." That's a lot better than being a fake underachiever, isn't it? But back to evaluation. You evaluate things (like a bicycle or a shirt) to see if you want to buy them or if they're worth the money. Evaluating is judging.

KIDS EVALUATING EACH OTHER

It's a little bit weird, but in this world (I haven't had a chance to spy on other worlds) everybody gets evaluated and everybody evaluates. It's almost a kind of revenge, isn't it? All day long, and I mean nonstop with no rest, kids evaluate each other—it's like they're trying to decide whether to buy or keep other kids as friends. It's just like picking out that new bike. What that means is that we are all forced to keep trying to sell ourselves to other kids. We try to seem right so that we can score high on other students' evaluations of us. That way they will accept and respect us as friends, or help make us popular, or prevent us from falling into total unpopularity. Sometimes I think kids don't even realize that they're spending their time and maybe also their money designing and advertising themselves. Imagine that I'm the local Jarvis salesman. I have to figure out how to get other kids to buy me:

Hey reader, did you ever think of yourself as a commercial for yourself?

Now, you might ask: how does Jarvis the Social Spy, a person who himself is a kid, know all this? The answer is that I've been watching these social commercials at Eastern Middle School with my own microscopic, evaluating, binocular, laser-sharp eyeball beams. Let me tell you about what I see when I watch other kids trying to seem to be something or someone.

For starters, there's this group of kids who sit together at lunch, and you see them grazing and cruising around town together sometimes on weekends. They sort of remind me of a herd of goats. They don't know that's what I call them; it's just my name for their gang. They really, really like each other, so they stick to their herd as if they need each other for protection. There are between eight and twelve of these goat kids, depending upon whether someone is home pretending to be sick or if someone has been kicked out for saying or doing something uncool. Kids can get back in the group if they wait a little while and then say they're sorry or do something extra wonderful for the others in the group. Your sly and a little shy spry spy, Jarvis, doesn't want to name any names because I am afraid I will make these kids hate me when they read this, and I might someday want to get in with them, although I doubt if they would ever let someone like me join their honorable herd. And also I really don't like those kids very much. But you never know.

LOOKING RIGHT AND DRESSING RIGHT

I have spied on the herd on several occasions. The very first thing I have noticed is that they all dress the same way. It's like they bought one set of clothes and had them photocopied. We don't have school uniforms at Eastern Middle School, but these kids have their own uniforms that have been given the OK by the bosses. The girls wear their hair almost the same, and the guys look as if they all ordered fake hair from the same catalog. They do a lot of talking at lunch, and they spend time discussing a very complicated and brainy subject: clothing. Yes, they sit around talking clothes talk. "Where did you get those shoes?" "That's a cool shirt; I have one just like it." "I really need some socks like that." I almost lost it the other day when two of the boys started talking about their boxer shorts in front of everyone—even the girls (who seemed very interested). I can assure you that Jarvis, your Social Spy, would never reveal such inside secrets to anyone except his mother, who knows anyway because she buys those things for him and even washes them. I feel a little embarrassed that she washes them, but maybe I'm too sensitive about body privacy. I discovered that not only do you have to wear the right clothes to stay with the herd but you also have to buy everything from the same store where everyone else gets their costumes. Now, if you ask me, that's like living under a dictator. It's not democratic. It goes against your basic right to buy whatever you want to wear wherever you want. But you know, those herd members look as if they are very happy to give up some rights and go along with the group.

Anyway, these goat-students really do worry about how they look. The other day I met two of the billy goats from the herd in the boys' room. I didn't go there to meet them; I went there because, well, you should be able to guess why I went there. It was one of my six trips a day (I seem to need to go more than most other kids). Anyway, while I was doing what I went there to do, which requires very little concentration most of the time, I watched these two guys in front of the sinks. They were both looking in the beautiful cracked mirrors that perfectly match the very attractive cracked walls, floors, ceilings, and windows of Eastern Middle School. Yes, the herd guys stood there fixing up their hair, as if they were about to walk out on a stage in front of a thousand screaming fans. Then they backed up to check out their upper bodies, then they moved back in again for hair close-ups. These kids were totally into how they looked. It was as if that's all they had to think about.

I have to tell you, reader, I don't much like looking in mirrors; I'd rather take my chances on how I look. But you know what? I think all the mirror gazing works for these guys. They are very popular. They have lots of friends. They are important and respected members of their herd, and a lot of students who are not lucky enough to be in the herd admire the ones who are. And these herd members look good just about all the time. They never, ever have a bad hair day! It probably takes them an hour or more to get dressed in the morning 'cause they have to check every little shirt wrinkle really carefully. The average dressing time for me is under three minutes on a slow day. Oh, by the way, I'm sure you are wondering why I am focusing on the boys in the herd. It's partly because this spy is not permitted where the girls go to check themselves out in broken mirrors. But I am absolutely positive that these girls spend just as much time checking out and changing how they look. Who knows, they may even spend more! Now, don't get me wrong. I think it's OK to want to look good. I just don't know how much you should think about it and how much time and worry should be spent on looking right in order to seem right. I also wonder if spending too much time on your body makes your mind rot. Who knows?

Now, I have to tell you about two kids at Eastern who are just the opposite of the ones in the goat herd. The first is a girl named Noriko. I talked about her a little bit before. Now, this girl loves horses. I bet she likes horses more than people. I can kinda understand that. Every day after school she gallops over to visit her horse, love it to death, and ride it. And every day she comes to school looking as if she just came back from a slumber party in her horse's stall. I mean, she is a mess, a total and complete mess of a mess. She never brushes her hair, which looks as if it has knots and kinks and dirt balls in it, and she wears the same torn red shirt every day with the same khakis—I can tell because the hole near her knee is always in the same place. Isn't that outstanding social spying? Anyway, one thing is very obvious: Noriko doesn't care about how she looks. She couldn't care less. Now, I know it's not nice to call someone a slob, but Noriko kinda makes you want to use that unkind word. Man, no one who cares about how she looks could look as grossly grungy as Noriko. Also, you know what? She's always by herself. She has no friends. No herd has ever heard of her (sorry about that one). I keep wishing she would find other girls or guys like herself; they could form their own we-don't-care-how-we-look herd.

OK, here's the other kid I want to tell you about. His name is Ryan, and every day he comes to Eastern Middle School wearing a tie and a blue or white shirt and a dark blue blazer with gold buttons on it. His black shoes are always so polished that you can see your face in them. Now, you should realize, reader, that wearing a tie at Eastern Middle School is almost as unusual as coming to school completely naked. Ryan may be the only student who even owns a tie. Other kids make fun of the way he dresses, but Ryan ignores them. And you know what? Ryan's brother Harry doesn't ever wear ties to school. So it isn't as if Ryan's parents make him wear a tie. He just does, and he doesn't care what anyone thinks. Every single day this kid looks as if he is paying a visit to Eastern Middle School from some other country somewhere, or else like he's a narcotics inspector, or maybe even a spy (but definitely not a Social Spy). Many times Ryan has explained that he really likes the way he looks when he's dressed like that. I can't decide if this kid is completely weird or if we should admire Ryan for looking the way he wants to look and not caring even the slightest tiny little bit what anybody else thinks about him. You know, I like Ryan—a lot.

By now, most of you are yawning, checking out your fingernails, clipping your toenails, staring out the window, or all of the above. So, this sounds like a very good time to turn the spotlight on our super-brilliant social expert (at least that's what he told me to write), Dr. Mel Levine (who dresses in totally boring clothes like your typical doctor).

• DR. LEVINE'S COMMENTS ON LOOKING RIGHT •

Jarvis's spy work has shown us three different ways kids deal with how they look. The students in that herd Jarvis spied on like to dress a certain way so that they can fit in with each other. They are very careful about where they buy their clothes and what they wear each day. They think a lot about their clothes and how to wear them. Then there's Noriko, the girl who loves horses.

She couldn't care less! Clothing means nothing to her. You can be sure she never even thinks about what she wears. She thinks looks are unimportant. But she has no friends. Is that because she prefers horses? Or is she a friend to horses only because she can't make friends with other kids? Or are there some other reasons why Noriko has no friends? Finally, we have Ryan, who dresses like a grown-up and wears a tie and jacket to school. He likes looking that way and doesn't care what others think. It probably does cost him some friendships, yet you have to give him credit for knowing what he likes and sticking with it. Is he stubborn, or is he a hero for being himself even if it means that other kids make fun of him?

In every school and in every country, how you dress seems to say something about who you are and also about the kind of group you want others to think you belong with. Some kids and also some grown-ups are extremely careful about how they dress. It's more than just wanting to look nice. They want others to think they are a certain kind of person, and their clothing and even their hair are supposed to make everyone think of them that way.

SELF-MARKETING

Your appearance is one part of marketing yourself. *Marketing* is a business word. When a company wants to sell a product, like a new car, their marketing department figures out how to make it look right and how to show it to people so that they will want to buy it. Well, every one of us is trying to sell a product. We are trying to sell ourselves to others. But we don't all market ourselves in the same way. And we are not all equally interested in marketing ourselves. For example, Noriko isn't too concerned about getting others to accept her. The kids in the herd, on the other hand, are very concerned, maybe even too concerned, with marketing themselves to each other. Then you have Ryan, who wants to market himself, but he's not trying to appeal to the "cool kids." He is trying to look like a very mature and neatly dressed person. I think Ryan is more interested in marketing himself to his teachers than to his fellow students at Eastern Middle School. That's his choice. When Jarvis told us about his ad, he was thinking about how kids market themselves to each other.

There are some other important aspects of marketing yourself and seeming right. These include your physical appearance (aside from your clothes and hairdo), how you move around, the interests you have, and what you do well. I know Jarvis has found out some interesting things about these parts of what we call *self-marketing* issues.

TAKING YOUR BODY TO SCHOOL

This is your favorite underachiever who has been told six thousand times that he would do better in school if he would only try harder, but who knows he would only try harder if he did better. Anyway, it's Jarvis, back from sneaking around and snooping in all the social corners and friendly dumpsters at Eastern Middle School. I am now ready to tell the world out there a very, very basic thing that I have found out. Now, this may sound really dumb and obvious to all of my overachieving readers, but I have discovered that kids are required to take their bodies to school with them. Not just their brains, but their bodies too. What a bummer, especially in middle school when that "bod," all those bones and organs shrink-wrapped in your skin, can cause you to worry all day. Sometimes you can't stop thinking about your body and how it affects how you seem to other people and also even more how you *think* you seem to others. Let me explain what I mean.

There's a kid at Eastern Middle School whose name is Jarvis Clutch (that's me, in case you forgot). You see, every once in a while I think it's a pretty good idea to spy on myself. Anyway, I am going through this difficult time of life that Dr. Levine and other grown-ups in authority like to call *puberty* (a very ugly-sounding word, in my opinion). During this confusing time, I keep noticing my body changing in ways that I am too embarrassed to describe on these pages. I am sure that other kids are having exactly the same wonderful, exciting, fascinating, scary, and disgusting experiences. Most of the time, it's fun and interesting to watch yourself grow up. Maybe that's one reason why so many of us really do care about how we look. We want to move things along and look as grown-up as we can as soon as possible. Well, one thing that happens just to make life difficult for us at a time when we want to look like gods is this cruel, uglifying disease called *acne* that some of us get, including Jarvis Clutch, a Social Spy with one to three small pimples on his face most days. This is what happens to me: I wake up in the morning and go wash my face and brush my teeth (soon I'm gonna add shaving to these awful chores). While washing my face, I look in the mirror (which has no cracks in it) and see a red, oily, insect-like invader under my skin on the tip of my nose. I rub it with a washcloth to see if I can wipe out the enemy, but that seems to make it angrier. Then I try putting some of my brother's pimple medicine on it, which makes it look worse because then people can tell you're trying to cover it up. Then I go to school, and all day long I keep thinking about it. I sit there in class with my hand covering the front of my nose. I feel sure that everyone is looking at that gross lump getting bigger and easier to spot by the second. Probably they are all talking about the thing on my nose behind my back; maybe they're even talking about it in front of my front! I wonder if I am being punished for something I did or said or ate. I hate the thing. That stupid zit ruins my whole day. It's something I can't control. It means I'm out of control. Kids my age like everyone to think they are in control of everything, and pimples are there to prove they aren't. It's an unfair, dirty trick. I guess I do care about how I look to others because I am jealous of all kids who have no pimples. Life's a lot easier for them.

That's enough of Jarvis spying on himself and his oily skin. But while we're getting too personal, I have to mention another thing about seeming right. At Eastern Middle School, different kids mature at different speeds. We have some eighth graders who look like sixth graders and some sixth graders who look like eighth graders. If you're one of the lucky ones, you look your age. The age you look can make a difference socially, especially if you're really small and immature. For example, there's this kid named Jeff, who is very small. If you saw him at the supermarket, you would think he was about nine years old, or even younger. I'm sure he's normal because they taught us in our health class that a lot of kids mature slowly and end up as tall as anyone else. For now, at least, he is short, and I am pretty sure that he has not yet reached puberty or even come close. In science class, Jeff sits between Rich, who looks as if he's a sixteen-year-old golf pro, and Madeleine, who looks like she could be Jeff's mom. But you know they're all the same age. You have to feel sorry for Jeff, but he seems to pretend that he's no different from other students. I spied on Jeff to see how he protects himself. First, he laughs when-ever kids make fun of his size or call him "shrimp." Second, he has appoint-ed himself our class comedian (which sometimes gets him into trouble, but he acts as if he doesn't care, and that seems cool to a lot of kids). He walks around with the top three buttons of his shirt unbuttoned so you can see a lot of his bony chest. And he makes sure you can see the red polka dot elastic of his boxer shorts above his belt. It's as if Jeff is shouting out at us: "I, Jeff, the little squirt, am proud of myself and my body. I'm cool and I'm not trying to hide anything from anybody. I'm small and immature, but I don't care." Unfortunately, reader, Jarvis the Social Spy cannot get inside of any of the kids he spies on. Does Jeff really feel OK about himself? Or is he very sad and scared inside? Whatever the truth is, Jeff puts on a good show. He's a great actor. It seems to work for him, but he probably wishes that he didn't have to put on an act.

So, you can see how our bodies play tricks on us and can make school life extrahard, especially since other kids are evaluating us and our bodies all the time. But a lot of times, your body cooperates and helps you seem right. There are lots of really beautiful girls and very good-looking guys who almost automatically become popular because they have faces and bodies everyone admires. Sometimes that makes your Social Spy fuming mad. Why should some people be accepted and respected just because they inherited good looks? It was just luck. And why should kids who aren't good-looking have trouble seeming right and getting popular? It doesn't seem fair. Good-looking kids make friends and get a good reputation much more easily. There's no doubt about it.

I need to tell you something very sad that I have seen in the lunchroom at school. I know this girl named Padma, and I feel really sorry for her. I think about two years ago she got in a car wreck. Her dad and her little brother were killed when the car caught on fire. She and her mom lived through it. But Padma got really bad burns all over her body. She had to have loads of operations, and now her face looks really bad. It's all scarred, and she's got a fake plastic lip that's too big and doesn't look real. Padma is a nice girl. She's a good student and never makes any trouble. But I have noticed at lunch that a lot of students try not to sit near her. They act as if they don't want to have to look at her face. Honestly, I don't much like looking at her either. But I have to tell you, sometimes I sit next to her because no one else will, and I force myself to look right at her while I talk to her. And you know, I'm starting to get used to how she looks; it doesn't bother me as much as it did before. I haven't told this to anyone, but for some reason, I don't know why, all of a sudden I start thinking about Padma just out of the blue—even in the middle of the night when I can't sleep (which is almost every night). Or, it could happen while I'm having breakfast, or just doing nothing. But I think about her and how sorry I feel for her. It's extremely strange. It really bothers me a lot. You know, it's almost like I feel guilty because my face isn't scarred and hers looks so awful. I know it's not my fault, but I feel a little guilty anyway. Does that make any sense? Maybe not, but that feeling won't go away.

HOW YOU MOVE AROUND

Now, here's another scientific breakthrough from the amazing, brilliant eyes of Jarvis the Social Spy. I have found that even the way students move their bodies can make a big social difference. Take this kid Trevor, who is really hyper. I mean, his body engines never cool off. He is like a jet-powered racecar on an icy racetrack, speeding down the corridor near the front entrance of Eastern Middle School. And that Trevor-car has no steering wheel and no brake pedal. It just zooms all around and seems to bounce off the walls. And when Trevor talks to you, he gets really close, too close and physical. He doesn't mean to, but he blocks your way and bumps into you like a football player. There's something about his crazy, reckless way of moving around that really bugs everyone. I think kids avoid Trevor because of the way he drives his body.

Here's another example. Her name is Emma, and she is clumsy, and I mean totally clumsy. She waddles around like a very awkward duck. She's a pretty OK person, but she always does things like trip when she gets off the bus, drop her papers in puddles, and spill juice on the shirt of the person next to her. She is so klutzy that it really affects how she looks. Can you believe that? Anyway, the way they both move—Emma like a hundred-year-old elephant with a sprained ankle and sore knees, and Trevor like wildfire—makes both of them seem kind of ugly in a way. I don't know why. I don't think it's fair. It shouldn't even matter. But it does. They're not liked much.

Now, here's my last example. There's this girl Cherise who never looks at anyone when she talks. I think she's a little shy. But I have noticed that whenever she talks to anyone, she never makes eye contact with the person she's talking to. For that little reason, I think that Cherise has lost some social points in the sometimes much too mean game of social life. It seems that little body movements like looking at the other person, moving your hands, or shrugging your shoulders in certain ways have something to do with what people think of you. I don't know why; it doesn't make a lot of sense to me, but these things matter.

I also feel very sorry for Hannah, who I talked about before. She is probably very used to being made fun of. You see, Hannah must weigh 175 pounds— at least. And I shouldn't say this or write this, but Hannah has all this black hair on her arms and her legs. I don't like looking at it, but sometimes I can't stop staring and wondering how all those dark hairy weeds grew there. Is she turning into a guy or something? Hannah is a generous girl from what I can tell. She does OK in school. She is super polite and never gets into fights or argues with anyone. She wears nice clothes and has a trendy haircut. That doesn't do much good, in my opinion. She still looks bad whatever she does. No one sits next to her at lunch or on the bus. There's really no room for anyone to sit. That must be so embarrassing. It almost makes me want to cry if I think about it too much. I would hate to be Hannah. A few weeks ago, all the girls had to climb ropes in P.E. You should have seen poor Hannah trying to get up that rope. I thought she was going to break the rope or else fall off and fracture her back or her entire skull. Some kids laughed, and it looked to me like the teacher was laughing a little too. How can people be so cruel? Hannah can't help the fact that she's so fat. No one could pull all that weight up a rope. And her weight seems to be making it hard for Hannah to have a reasonable reputation and some friends at Eastern Middle School, even though her social cognition is probably OK.

BODY ATTACHMENTS

Now, to change the subject, I have to tell you what some kids go through to seem right, or, as Dr. Levine would say, to market themselves. Jarvis the Social Spy recently completed a scientific survey in the completely foul-smelling lunchroom at Eastern Middle School. I wanted to find out how many students had made big-time body additions (most likely trying to seem right to other kids). Well, here are the results, hot off the press: I spotted eleven boys with one or two earrings and seven students with rings in their noses—

ouch! I was not permitted to check out all 230 belly buttons, so I have no information about that, but I may do a survey at the swimming pool next summer. I counted eleven tattoos and thirty-three kids with dyed hair, including several with purple hair, some with yellow hair, and a couple with both! And guess what? This probably won't surprise you, but the ones who had added the most hardware to their bodies seemed to be friends and were sitting together at lunch. It was as if those body attachments were required to be part of some groups (or herds).

Now, I'm not going to say what I think about body attachments because it is important for different people to have different tastes. To tell you the truth, I've given some thought to punching a hole in one of my own precious earlobes. The idea is currently under consideration. For one thing, my older brother Jeremy is such a straight arrow that it looks as if his joints don't bend. He does everything well and loves to impress my mother, his teachers, and our completely uninteresting neighbors. I can't even begin to do as well as he does in school. So maybe I'll wear a huge earring. Does that make any sense to you? It does to me. It would put me in a completely different league from my brother and then maybe people would stop comparing us.

I've asked a couple of kids why they do things like pierce their body parts or dye their hair purple or yellow, and they all say the same thing: "I just like the way it looks." I don't know whether to believe them or not. Do they really and truly like it or do they like the way it makes them seem right to others? Is it a way to market themselves—so it doesn't really matter whether deep down inside they like it or don't like it? Who knows, I'm just a Social Spy, not some kind of shrink.

The kids who don't have tattoos and things you stick in holes still seem to think about how their bodies look all the time. I mean, that seems to be all they ever think about. They don't care how their brain is doing as long as their body looks slick. There's this girl Irene who is afraid to eat anything because she might gain half an ounce. At lunch the other day, her fantastic feast was about 45 percent of one skinny carrot. One of her friends told me that Irene skips breakfast and doesn't exactly stuff herself at supper or pig out between meals (except for the occasional half grapefruit that she shares with two friends of hers). I'm no medical freak, but I'm sure that's wrecking her health and that eating like that could cause big problems for her someday. Guys think a lot about their bodies, too. I know some boys who spend hours and hours lifting weights and working out so that they can have these mega-muscles on their chests and abs. Don't get me wrong; I think it is great to exercise and stay in shape, and I think it's good to keep your bod in decent shape and not eat huge overdoses of greasy, grimy foods and spend your life watching TV and playing video games, keeping your muscles out of work. But there are some students at Eastern Middle School who overdo all that body-care stuff. In the opinion of your very observant Social Spy, these kids don't just exercise or eat right to feel healthy and have a heart that pumps blood well, they do it mostly because they want to appear gorgeous and impressive to everybody. They feel like they have to show off their bodies.

I feel bad for them.

HOW SPORTS CAN MAKE YOU SEEM RIGHT

Reader, I have found out that it's not just how you look but also what you do that can make a big difference in the fierce social game. Sports are probably the best example I can think of. Kids who are athletes get a free pass to popularity; it's a lot easier for them than it is for kids who are always chosen last for teams in P.E. At least here in Eastern Middle School, almost everyone seems to worship the football players, the guys and the girls on the basketball teams, and other sports idols. Take Jake. He's the fourteen-year-old football quarterback on our middle school team. To me, he looks as if he's about twenty-two years old. He is as handsome as those perfect plastic kids wearing the latest styles in department store windows. Being so good-looking helps his popularity, of course, and they say he will be able to go to any college on a football scholarship. If he decides not to go to college, he could always enter beauty contests or become a lifeguard. Jake is quiet, but he's also kind of a snob, you know, totally stuck-up. Girls in little swarms and sometimes even medium-sized swarms buzz all around Jake in school. They remind me of the fleas that bug my German shepherd. I can tell that Jake loves all the attention he gets. I spy on him and wonder what it would be like to be Jake instead of Jarvis. Would I switch with him if I could? Probably, at least for a few weeks. It's like he could have anything he wants. He could win any election, get invited to any party, and have any friends he could ever want. He's got loads of power. We might all want power, but it seems that only a few of us can actually have it.

Then there's Thomas, whose glasses are so thick that I feel sorry for his nose. He had a perfect record a few years ago on our Little League baseball team. He struck out every single time he came up, and every single ball that came to him in right field went over him or under him or through him as if he wasn't even there. I really respect kids who are that consistent. They never let

you down! You won't be surprised when I tell you that Thomas despises sports. It's hard to like something that causes you to get embarrassed all the time. He has a way of not dressing down for P.E. class—like me. Then he gets these threatening letters from the teacher for this evil crime (almost as serious as chewing gum while marching). But would you want to go to P.E. and be laughed at every day? Anyway, Thomas is a fantastic chess player, and he collects old coins from Asia or someplace like that. He is very interested in ancient history and is lucky enough to have class with a very ancient history teacher here in the old ruins we call Eastern Middle School, historic site of the world's earliest boys' room plumbing. Thomas is definitely not a popularity king. You don't see attack squads of girls hunting down Thomas the way they chase Jake, and Thomas is a much better student. I also think (although no one ever asks my opinion) that Thomas is a more interesting and intelligent person than Jake. It's just that at our school, Jake seems to be a product that's much easier to market than Thomas. But you know what? Thomas has a couple of really close friends. They play video games and chess a lot. They really don't care what everyone else thinks. By the way, Thomas is one of my friends.

WHAT YOU LIKE TO DO AND WHAT YOU DO WELL

As you know, people in our school really look up to the star athletes. Chess players or teenagers who get all excited over collecting moths don't stand a chance—no matter how good they are at their hobby, at least not here at good old jock-worshipping Eastern Middle School. You see, it's not just being really good at something that gets you respect and friendship from other kids, it's also the activities you choose to do. Some activities are acceptable, but other things you like can make you a total social outcast. So, if you have two pet pythons at home (which I do) or if you are a guy who takes ballet lessons (which I don't) or a girl who builds fortresses for her pet hermit crabs out of mud and rocks in her backyard, you may find yourself all by yourself. But if you ask me, some of the most popular kids could be on Jarvis's anti-honor roll, limited to those special students who have the highest bore score in the school! So we can add the things you're good at (like sports) and the things you enjoy doing (not counting going on six-hour moth hunts) to the list of things that make you seem right (or wrong).

Now readers, you might be asking yourselves, what about kids who are really brainy, the ones who get straight As in school and work very hard and study really hard for tests and hand in every single homework assignment on time or maybe even two days early? Are they liked or are they rejected? What do you think? Well, it all depends on a lot of things, including many of the social cognition ingredients you have already read about. If you get all As plus you have outstanding social cognition, other kids will be nice enough to excuse you for getting good marks. Whew! But if you are a brain with social cognition that's not so great, you'd better watch out because you are skating on popularity thin ice, and a lot of kids seem to think that getting good grades isn't all that cool.

YOUR NEED TO SEEM COOL

Speaking of being cool, socially climbing reader, now I get to tell you about a discussion that took place in our health class a few weeks ago. You see, there's this slightly sickly-looking man, Mr. Prince (probably married to little old Mrs. Princess), who teaches us unsanitary, diseased, smelly eighth graders how to stay as unhealthy as possible so that we can lead very short but happy lives. Just kidding. This very overweight, out-of-shape, million-calorie-eating health teacher not only helps us worry about how we are wiping out our bodies by eating too much and sleeping too little, he's also into such killer topics as sex, drugs, alcohol, and what he calls *mental health*. We have all kinds of discussions about mental health because Mr. Prince wants us to know more about our minds so that we can tell when we're losing them. Anyway, one day Mr. Prince was talking about the importance of having friends (I was wondering whether he had any). He wanted to know if there was anything bothering us about friends or about social life. So your very own Jarvis, always trying to get great stuff for this book, jumped up and said, "Mr. Prince, I would like us to talk about what it means to be cool. Everyone uses the word and lots of kids want to get called cool, but I don't understand what it really means." Mr. Prince answered, "Jarvis, maybe you're wondering because no one has ever accused *you* of being cool!" Everyone in the class laughed. I thought to myself, "That Mr. Prince is such a wonderful comedian. I wonder who writes his unfunny lines." "But sure," Mr. Prince announced, "why don't we talk about that for a little while?" So I took out my un-trusty, rusty recorder and stored up a bunch of things that different kids said about what other kids do that lets us say that they are cool:

• One girl shouted, "When you're cool, you act as if nothing bothers you and no one can hurt you. You seem really brave and, in a way, tough."

• A kid in the back put in his two cents worth. "I think being cool is just being very relaxed, completely, 125 percent relaxed most of the time. You walk around relaxed. You sit on the floor in front of your locker or at your desk as if you are a finalist in a relaxation tournament. You stretch your legs out in a certain way and lean on things and stand a little crooked just to prove how relaxed you are. When you lose it and stop being relaxed, your friends all tell you that you've blown your cool!"

• Another girl stuck in, "And when you're cool, you do some risky things, some stuff you probably shouldn't do that you can't really get in serious trouble for—maybe like using bad words or smoking or something like that."

• The guy who sits next to me blurted out, "When you're cool, you're really very normal in how you like look and act but you do little things that make you just a little different from anyone else—not too different, but just the right amount different in ways that are neat."

• One boy, not known around Eastern for making the most brilliant or prizewinning comments, said, "When you're a cool person it's because you say and do cool things."

• Another one of my brilliant, social genius classmates added "And someone who's cool knows how to walk right, like in the hallways or at the mall."

• Finally, one boy told the class, "To be cool, you have to do cool things, even if sometimes you don't want to or it's against your better judgment or even against your parents. That's how I got started smoking. I wanted to be cool, and smoking was an easy way to do something cool. Now I can't stop, and I'm not sure being addicted to something is too cool."

So you can see, reader, coolness is cool. A lot of kids I know must spend most of their time trying to figure out how to seem cool. They want to be cool, look cool, listen to cool music, say cool things, and eat cool pizza with everything on it, which may not be truly cool unless it's hot! A lot of these kids have to be careful they don't get caught doing something that's definitely not cool—like maybe studying very hard for a test. You know, students' grades can drop because they'd rather seem cool than smart. I know this guy who studies secretly. He hides out so that his cool friends won't find out he's working hard to do well in school. How do you feel about that, reader? By the way, every school must have kids in it who really don't care if they're cool or not. It's too bad they can't all go to the same school—Uncool Middle School, a place where no kids seem right and no kids care that they don't seem right. Everyone just wants to be himself or herself. That's not so bad, I guess.

The word *cool* means different things to different people. Some of the common characteristics of someone who might be called cool are shown in this diagram. Do you agree with these characteristics?

HOW DO YOU SEEM COOL?

It looks as if most things don't bother you.

You do some risky things.

You have some smooth ways of walking and talking.

You Seem to Be Cool

You have at least one strength that people admire (like looks or athletic ability).

You are supernormal, not weird.

You dress a certain way.

You look really relaxed.

You're accepted by at least one group.

One social thermometer kids use to judge each others' coolness is music. What you listen to or don't listen to can really influence what other kids think of you. I don't want to say very much about music, even though I really like music a lot. Everyone knows that music affects your social life. I see kids who spend hours and hours listening to music, talking about music, or going to dances or concerts and stuff like that. Now, if you happen to be a kid who doesn't like the same music that some other kids like, you could easily be considered highly weird or totally screwed up in your tastes. Jarvis, the Social Spy, has faced this crisis himself, but I'm not gonna tell you what kind of music I like to listen to, at least not yet.

POSERS AND POSING AND COMPOSING YOUR POSING

While we're talking about being cool and seeming right, I want to teach Dr. Levine a word he might not have in his oversized medical vocabulary. I don't think he knows what a poser is. A *poser* is a kid who does things and moves around in a certain way just to seem cool. Everyone does this sometimes, but posers can't stop posing. That's why they are called posers! They overdo it; they can't compose their pose right (I thought of that and I think it's very clever). There's this kid named Achir here at Eastern. He loves to skateboard with his buddies. I've noticed that they always skateboard in public where everyone can see them. Achir and the other skaters love showing off for the rest of us. When you see Achir in front of the lockers, he's usually doing high jumps, proving to everyone he thinks is watching him how he can touch the ceiling easily. When he's not doing that, he's tossing his books in his locker to impress us with what a good shot he is and how he doesn't really care if he totals his notebook. He also puts his body in special mighty positions, so that he looks like the Statue of Liberty or something. By the way, we have just as many female posers as male posers in this school. And you know, probably everybody is a poser some of the time. A little posing is good. It can let you try on different disguises to find out how they make you feel and how other people react to them. You know what I mean? But there are kids out there who can't stop posing. They are bad at composing their posing (still very clever). They make me nervous.

We are lucky enough to have at our school two full-time poster posers, Zach and Molly. Remember them? They are both very near the top of the Eastern Middle School popularity chart, and what I didn't mention before is that they seem to love each other madly other or something. What bugs me is that they make such a big show about it. They want everyone to see them walking really close together with their arms around each other, holding hands, or even hugging where everyone can walk by and see them in action. If you ask me, I think they're mostly posers, trying to look ultracool. They hope kids who don't have a girlfriend or boyfriend will feel jealous, I think. In a way, I feel sorry for them. They probably can't tell the difference between who they really are and who they want other people to think they are. Hey! I think I just wrote something brilliant. They don't seem to know how to just be themselves without putting on a public show. They could love each other in private—I've heard that a lot of people do that. But then, it could be that Jarvis, your Social Spy, is just a little bit jealous of Zach and Molly.

Here's something for all you readers to puff on: cigarette smoking. Smoking is another form of posing, and we have a surprising number of loyal smokers in my grade. I spied on and interviewed smokers for a few days a few months ago. I asked some of them how they got started. You know, they all said pretty much the same thing. They started because smoking looked "really cool." But a big part of the coolness of smoking is that it makes you look older, like some kind of an adult-type. They try to hold and move the dumb cigarette in a really smooth way—like someone who's been puffing away for fifteen years or more. Now, reader, that's just plain a little bit slightly weird. I see so many adults, including teachers in this perfectly perfect school, who spend all their time trying to look younger, and here we have all these kids trying to look older. Everyone wants to change places. What's wrong with looking your age? I don't know; maybe that's a dumb question. But I have to tell you, watching kids smoke is something else. They look so relaxed and they smoke so smoothly and casually, you'd think that they had been smoking for years and years—even while their parents were changing their diapers. Smoking makes kids look not just like an imitation adult but like people who have been very grown-up adult for ages and are very used to moving their hand (with a cigarette in it) around in a super-smooth, totally grown-up way. Then, of course, smoking gets to be a habit you can't kick, and maybe you get cancer in your lungs or a messed-up heart from it, and then you're lying in a hospital bed very deathly sick, and what do you think about? You think about how awesome it would be to be young again, to be an eighth grader at Eastern Middle School. Oh no! Kids will kill themselves to seem cool!

Reader, I'm ready to cool it on the subject of coolness. How am I doing, Dr. Levine? Do I have X-ray social vision? Have I said some things about seeming right that seem right to you? Anyhow, now it's your chance to pose, and to impress our readers with your amazing insight.

• ON THE IMAGE YOU SHOW TO OTHERS AND YOUR OWN SELF-IMAGE •

Jarvis continues to make important observations about the social scene at Eastern Middle School. I'm sure most of these things could be seen at schools everywhere. Jarvis has made some good points about appearances. Somehow, the way you look and the way you move around affects how other people see you, which influences whether they accept you and how they think about you. I'm sure we all agree with Jarvis that sometimes these judgments can be unfair. If a person looks awkward when moving around, it's certainly not that person's fault. Also, what kids said in Jarvis's quotes about coolness are very important. Coolness has come up in every school I have ever been to. Often kids talk about being cool without figuring out all the different meanings of the word. Seeming cool (if that's how they want to seem) can be pretty natural for some people. But in every school there are many students with weaknesses in their social cognition who would like to be cool, but can't ever quite pull it off. When they try to be cool, either they overdo it and look silly or they just can't give off the cool signals at all. They may over-sell themselves, and try too hard to seem right, which then prevents them from really seeming right. They become posers, and it can be very easy to see through their poses. A good friend or an adult might need to coach them on how to act cool or help them realize that in some cases it's actually cooler not to even try to be cool!

In previous chapters, we discussed the importance of self-monitoring, of knowing how you're doing with other people. This ability is essential when it comes to knowing how you seem to other kids. Do you know how you're coming across? Do you think everyone thinks you're a really neat person when, in reality, they think you are odd or totally out of it? Whether we know it or not, each of us has an image that others get to know when they get to know us. We say that people *project* an image of themselves. Some of us project more than one image; we may seem one way with one particular group of people (like teachers), but project a different image with another group (like the members of your Scout troop). We also have a *self-image,* which is the image we have of our own selves. That self-image may or may not be the same one that other people have of us. By knowing how you seem to others, you have a chance to make some changes in your image projection if you can and if you decide you want to. You could decide, "I think I need to seem more like a serious student" or "I think I want to be more of a party kid" or "I want to seem more grown-up." To make this kind of image change, you have to ask two important questions: What image do I have now? and, What image would I like to have?

• • •

THE IMPORTANCE OF SEEMING COOL

Not everyone cares about seeming cool. But some kids think about it very often, and they work pretty hard to seem cool as often as possible. You can see in this diagram that different kids feel differently about how important being cool is to them and how much they want to work on seeming cool. Where would you place yourself on the social thermometer?

NOT COOL — I try not to be cool.

— I'm not cool and it doesn't matter to me.

KIND OF COOL — I want to be cool some of the time.

— I try hard to seem cool.

COOL — I'll do almost anything to make other kids think I'm cool.

WHEN SOMEONE CAN'T SEEM TO SEEM RIGHT

Sometimes on the social scene, kids forget to look beneath the image of a person. So, some terrific kids may not seem right, but they may have great strengths that just aren't visible. Some kids may be really kind, interesting, talented, and ready and able to be someone's best friend, but because these kids don't seem right when you look at them, and because they don't show a certain kind of image, they may not even be given a chance to experience what it's like to be liked. There's a lesson in that: we have to look for and appreciate the qualities people have that you can't see. Those qualities are more important than images.

As you might guess, students who have a hard time seeming right even when they want to can become very unhappy and feel extremely lonely. Hopefully, such kids have one or two good friends who accept them as they are. But some kids who can't seem to seem right don't have any friends. The problem becomes especially serious when students are made fun of continuously because they don't seem right. We all get teased occasionally, and that's OK, even fun. But someone who is overweight, or looks much younger than he really is, or has a very large nose, or clumsy muscle coordination may be laughed at, called names, and embarrassed frequently because of something he or she has no control over. Obviously, that's downright cruel, but it happens just about every day in just about every school. Most of the time kids who are made fun of frequently or called names try to act as if they don't care. They may even laugh or just walk away when embarrassed in front of a crowd of kids. But I can tell you as a doctor who has known many of those students, that down deep in their hearts, they feel terrible pain, really terrible. Even though they may look and act as if it doesn't bother them at all, being made fun of day after day ignites a fire within them. All of the teasing and taunting can permanently wreck their self-esteem and make them feel as if they are inferior to everyone else. In the worst cases, after many, many bouts of teasing, the fire inside burns out of control, and kids can turn violent or even do very bad things to other kids or to themselves—as if to get revenge for years of being put down in public. So making fun of another person who can't seem to seem right is really like a kind of crime. It should never happen. Kids should discourage others from doing this in any way they can.

Now let's review the parts of seeming right that we have covered in this chapter. They are summarized in the box below.

BEING EVALUATED AND EVALUATING OTHERS

LOOKING RIGHT AND DRESSING RIGHT

MARKETING YOURSELF

TAKING YOUR BODY TO SCHOOL

MOVING AROUND THE RIGHT WAY

WHAT YOU ATTACH (OR DECIDE NOT TO ATTACH) TO YOUR BODY

WHETHER OR NOT YOU'RE AN ATHLETE

WHAT YOU LIKE DOING AND WHAT YOU DO WELL

YOUR NEED AND ABILITY TO SEEM COOL

YOUR TASTE IN MUSIC

COMPOSING YOUR POSING

YOUR SELF-IMAGE AND THE IMAGE YOU SHOW TO OTHERS

SELF-MONITORING HOW YOU SEEM

Now that we have considered the important ingredients of seeming right, we can move on in the next chapter to the second part of social cognition, which we will call *talking right*. That has to do with how you are able to use language well to interact with other people.

SOME SOCIAL QUESTIONS AND PROJECTS FROM THIS CHAPTER TO THINK ABOUT, DO, AND/OR DISCUSS

1. What kind of clothes do the popular kids wear at your school? How are their clothes different from other kids' clothes? Do kids who can't afford expensive, trendy clothes have trouble being popular?

2. How would you try to help a student who is being rejected because of the way he or she looks?

3. How does a student "market" himself or herself to others? Is it possible to overdo this? How would that seem?

4. Why do you think students get tattoos or piercings? How do you feel about these things—are they OK or bad and why?

5. Is it possible to have tastes (such as in music or clothing) that are different from everyone else's and still seem OK socially?

6. What does the word *cool* mean to you? Would you want to add to the discussion of coolness in this chapter?

7. If you had a brother or sister who definitely was not cool, what advice would you give him or her to become cooler?

8. How does getting good grades influence how cool you are at your school? Are kids who get good grades rejected, respected, or does it depend?

9. What does the word *eccentric* mean to you? Do you think that there are eccentric kids?

10. If you were running a middle school, what would you do to prevent kids from making fun of students who can't seem to seem right?

11. What words do you think other kids would use in describing how *you* seem to them (e.g., funny, friendly, a little strange, quiet, etc.)?

12. Are there some observations Jarvis makes in this chapter that would never be seen at your school? Are there some parts of seeming right at your school that are not covered in this chapter? What are they?

★ JARVIS PROJECTS FOR CHAPTER 3 ★

Writing Project 1: Make up an advertisement for yourself, one that lets kids know why they should like you and accept you into their social group. Include your social strengths and anything else about you that you think they would find cool. See my ad on page 66 for ideas. And be creative! Use the computer or art stuff to make your ad look like a winner.

Writing Project 2: Write about a day in the life of a student who might be called the most normal and uninteresting kid in your school. Then write a description of the most unusual (eccentric) kid in the school. Write about things like their interests, their tastes, their different appearances, and the way they dress and what they do. Then pick the kids you'd rather be like and tell why.

~ CHAPTER 4 ~
TALKING RIGHT

I've already told you that during my social studies (which are, of course, not the same as that astoundingly fascinating class called social studies) at Eastern Middle School, I used my ancient, antique, creaky-sneaky, fossilized tape recorder plus that fantastic headset called Jarvis's ears to tune in to what my fellow Eastern Middle School talkers were talking about, what they were saying to each other. Dr. Mel tipped me off that the way kids talk tells you lots about their social cognition. Remember that whole idea of social cognition that Levine used to impress us? It all has to do with how your mind does social thinking. Since the good doctor claims that talking right with other people takes pretty decent social cognition, I started to wonder if you can tell how much social success kids are having from the way they talk. I found out a lot just by tuning in and listening, and you, my fellow social student, will learn a lot from finding out what I found out a lot about. Remember: you heard all of this first from Jarvis Clutch—Social Spy.

WHEN YOU DON'T USUALLY SOUND RIGHT

Oh man, we've got some students here at Eastern who turn everybody off completely almost the second they open their mouths (except for when they're eating or breathing). A lot of these kids seem to talk OK in class—like when they're called on in English or math. But when they say things socially, when they speak to the rest of us, they sound like they've just fallen off some other planet. They are totally, I mean completely, totally, entirely out of it. Take Celine, a too-tall kid who would get only one vote (her own) in any school election. Here's a conversation I recorded between her and Katia, who is considered to be a truly cool girl—I'm sure you remember learning everything you'll ever need to know about what it means to be cool in the last chapter.

Katia: That test was so hard! I think I messed up. My mom's gonna kill me when she finds out.

Celine: Are you kidding? I thought it was a breeze. You must have some big leaks in your brain, and I mean huge holes.

Katia: I studied really hard, and now I'm worried. That was the final exam. It counts a lot!

Celine: I'm pretty sure I'm getting an A. I bet I did better than anyone else in the class. Mr. Jordan's gonna think I'm some kind of math genius. If you're really nice to me, I might be nice enough to help you with math, Katia, especially since your mind doesn't seem to be as intelligent as mine. I could explain it all to you, since you don't seem to get it on your own. Or you could just cheat.

Katia: Just because I had trouble on a math test doesn't mean my brain's dead. Everyone does badly sometimes—even you, Celine. I bet there are some things you've had serious trouble with at school.

Celine: No way! You don't know anything about me, or about how smart I am. I hate when kids like you think they know it all when they don't know anything.

That's so typical for Celine. She always sounds completely hateful and boastful. And you know what? She has no friends. If you ask my opinion (which no one has done for the last six years of my recorded history), Celine is not as mean, nasty, treacherous, angry, cruel, and generally gross as the other girls say she is. She just sounds that way! She doesn't even know how she sounds. That's her *social language* trouble acting up. Take the example I just gave you. I think Celine really likes Katia and would like to be her friend. But when she turns on that killer voice box of hers, the wrong feelings come shooting out, ones she doesn't mean. From the way she talks, you'd think she couldn't stand Katia. Maybe good old Dr. Levine can explain that to us later, but I have a feeling that Celine doesn't know how to pick the right words and get her voice to sound like a decent person's.

Now if we could give Celine a social language transplant, here's how she would sound:

Katia: That test was so hard! I think I messed up. My mom's gonna kill me when she finds out.

Celine: I know it was hard. But you're smart. I'm sure you'll do well on other tests. And I'm sure your mom will understand. Moms know that everyone messes up sometimes. If you want, we could study together for the next test. And maybe after that, my mom would take us to the mall.

My made-up version of Celine would fit her better. I happen to know that Celine is OK. She's even kind—at least to stray cats. She feeds all the strays in our neighborhood. I know because she lives across the street from me, and I've known her since we were little kids. You'd never guess how nice she is from how she speaks. She can't get her true good feelings into words, so she always sounds angry or snobby when she really isn't. Or she sounds as if she's bragging or criticizing or putting other people down all the time, but she never realizes that that's how she comes across. It's like she can't hear herself socially. So, she's got no friends, a bad reputation, and a telephone that never rings for her. Celine's 100 percent, completely rejected, mostly because of how she talks. The other thing about Celine is that she always sounds negative. I mean, she puts down everything and everybody. It's like she's so super-superior that she can criticize and tear everything and everybody around her to shreds. She doesn't have any idea how terrible she sounds.

By the way, speaking of my neighborhood, which I have named "Boreland" (best known for being the world's most unexciting, uninteresting, and especially un-unusual place to be forced to live), I have to tell you about an old man whose house is down the block from the Clutch family castle. This guy must be at least eighty-five years old. For all I know, he's 125. He lives all by himself, and everyone says he's very mean. His name is Mr. Crowly, and the kids all call him Mr. Growly. That's because he's super grouchy, and he sounds like a fierce growling tiger whenever you come near his property. But you know, I've been told that he gives a lot of money to poor people and to his church. I wonder if he's a little like Celine, a good person who just sounds vicious when he talks. He can't control the bad feelings that shoot out of his mouth like bullets. That's why people don't like him and think he's mean, even though I bet he has a good heart. I wonder how many old people lose their ability to put the right feelings into language?

CONVERSATIONAL SKILL

But getting back to kids, who are different from old people in some important ways (mainly they haven't been around as long), I have to tell you about another part of social language. This part has to do with knowing how to have a conversation with someone else, which is not the same as having a serious talk with yourself.

I have discovered that some people are great at conversation, and others are conversational dropouts. What I mean is that there are some things you have to do to be good at having conversations, and if you don't do these things, you get into conversational hot water. Listen to this terrible conversation that I recorded with Sen's permission:

Sen: There's this great new game I got called *Chopper Mania IV*. It's really cool. They have these supersonic, solar-powered helicopters with rotors that shoot off purple flames as they spin at astronomic speeds, faster than the speed of light, even faster than the speed of dark! You have to figure out how to intercept and bust the flame thrust.

Sydney: Yeah, that's like the game I got. I…

Sen: And I played with my brother; he couldn't bust a single thrust, and there I was whamming and slamming every flame, every one of them! ZOOM! Kerchoom! POW!

Sydney: Yeah, I like playing with my brother, too. I can beat him almost every time. I…

Sen: There was this one time when the rotors were going blazing fast and oh man, you shoulda seen how I zapped every flying flame—Whammo!—into the wild blue astro sky. Awesome, totally awesome.

Sydney: You must have really quick reflexes to do that. I know this kid who practices for like five hours a day, and he can beat almost anyone at *Dynamite the Termite*. He knows just where…

Sen: I love games. When I grow up, I want to be a game designer. I'll make millions and get paid for making and playing games. I'll also give game lessons. That would be so much fun, so excellent.

Sydney: Maybe I can be your partner. We can work together.

Sen: I'll be so rich that I'll be able to buy any game I want!

Sydney: I'd better get going now.

Did you catch that one-way conversation? Poor Sydney. As Sen walked away, Sydney told me that she couldn't stand him. When I asked why, Sydney shrugged her shoulders and said, "He talks too much and he only cares about himself."

It's true that Sen doesn't even know what a conversation is. He was talking as if he were the only person in the room. He never listened to anything Sydney said. He just kept talking and talking about himself, even boasting about himself without showing any interest in Sydney's ideas or reactions. Maybe that's one reason Sen has no friends. He doesn't know how to have a conversation with another person. He doesn't know that you have to listen, then talk, and attach some of your talking to what other people are saying to you. Sen fails at that, big-time, which guarantees that he will be a strong candidate to win the trophy as the most unpopular kid in the class! Poor guy. Whoever built his brain forgot to install the wiring for talking in a conversation!

But now friends and readers, it is time to hear from the crazy and wonderful world of the species known as adults. Dr. Mel Levine is set to write some words that will help us understand more about the talking parts of social thinking. But please don't close this book and toss it in the black hole you call your locker. I promise I'll be back soon.

• DR. LEVINE'S COMMENTS ON SOCIAL LANGUAGE •

Jarvis has uncovered some really important ideas about crucial parts of social language. First, in Celine we met a girl who sounded really mean and insensitive when she was talking to Katia. Katia felt pretty upset about how she had done on a test, yet Celine bragged about how well she had done. Celine spoke as if she was unaware of how Katia felt. She didn't try to make Katia feel good, and instead accused her of having an inferior mind. That was cruel. But there's a good chance that Celine didn't intend to be cruel and hostile. That's probably just the way she talks, which is a very serious problem for her because it means that nobody wants to be her friend. She certainly sounds mean, but doesn't mean to sound mean. In fact, Celine doesn't even know how mean she sounds. Then she wonders why she has no real friends. Actually, Celine likes Katia a lot, but she doesn't show it when she talks. So everyone thinks Celine doesn't like anyone because of the way she talks, and then they don't like her. What a trap she's in! Celine obviously has a problem with social language; she can't get her true feelings out when she speaks, so everyone misinterprets her feelings and attitudes.

Our friend Sen has a different kind of social language problem. He has no idea how to carry on a real two-way conversation. When you talk to another person, there is supposed to be some give-and-take. One person says something, and then the other person reacts to what the first person said, and then the first person says something connected to what the second person said about what the first person said. That's what a conversation is: sharing your thoughts with someone else who shares his or her thoughts with you. In Sen's case, he just kept talking without really listening or responding to what Sydney was trying to tell him. Also, Sen couldn't stop bragging about himself and never said anything to make Sydney feel good. And he didn't react when Sydney said anything. It was almost as if Sen were talking to himself. He didn't need anyone else around because he wasn't really participating in a conversation. Eventually, Sydney sensed this and got really annoyed with Sen. Yet Sen probably never realized how much he was boasting and ignoring what Sydney was trying to say. The sad part is that Sen really likes Sydney and wants to be her friend. Sen doesn't mean to do all the talking. He doesn't even realize that he talks so much. The words just keep coming. The fact that Sen talks too much without listening and responding to other peoples' ideas is really a problem with social language. All that one-way talking made Sen lose a possible friend. Whenever we're in a conversation, we all need to ask ourselves, "Am I doing too much of the talking?" That's a great question. By asking yourself that question and talking less if you need to, you can make conversations work a lot better.

Problems expressing yourself and problems with real conversation are major parts of the language side of social thinking. But some others aspects of talking count a lot too. Let's go back to Jarvis for more of his social language discoveries.

CODE SWITCHING

Hi folks. It's Jarvis here again to inform and entertain his crowds of thrilled, cheering fans out there in reader-land. I'm ready to tell you about some other social language things I found out and recorded on my trusty, rusty recorder. First of all, I have to tell you about Reginald, poor old Reginald Geranium (or something like that). This kid is some kind of genius, but other kids think he's weird, and you'll see why in a second. Reginald reminds me of the stuff you use to keep bugs off your skin; whenever he starts to talk, other kids want to fly away. He is a walking, talking kid repellent. His mouth is one big aerosol can. Listen to what he said the other day when some kids were describing their plans for the summer:

Reginald: This summer I want to learn more about paleontology. It is so interesting.

Alex: Pale-ee-in what?

Reginald: Paleontology. Everyone knows what that is; it's the scientific study of fossils, extinct animals, and related topics within that general domain. I've gotten especially absorbed by *Longisquama insignis*, which, as you know, is an archosaur from the late Triassic period, one that possesses wing-like appendages. So many misinformed paleontologists think that it is the ancestor of our contemporary birds. These creatures used to shed their scales, which might well be the forerunners of the modern-day feathers that we observe on birds. I really doubt it though, don't you? I mean, the earliest known bird was the archaeopteryx and that animal dates back 150 million years, so it actually came before *Longisquama insignis*. I think it would be inspiring to study all the fossils from different kinds of feathered creatures, don't you?

Reginald didn't even notice that Alex had flown away in the middle of his very long lecture on dead birds' feathers. If you ask me, Reginald sounded kind of extinct himself. He uses those grown-up words and always talks about things no one else is interested in. And he doesn't know when to lay off—he just keeps going. He thinks that if he is interested in something, everybody else must be too. Boy is he wrong about that!

Now, here's what Reginald had to say at lunch the same day:

Alex: I've been collecting those new quarters. I'm gonna try to get them all. They'll be worth a whole lot some day.

Reginald: I keep on making new discoveries about insects. Don't you think that insects are marvelous? I was just reading that insects have three pairs of legs that emanate from their thorax. One or two pairs of wings also branch off from this part of the insect's body. And, of course, insects possess many-segmented abdomens, which enclose their reproductive and digestive organs. Oops, I almost forgot those critical excretory organs, which are situated anatomically in proximity to all other essential organs. And everything, I mean everything, is apt to be protected in a surprisingly impervious exoskeleton.

To be honest with you, tired reader of this tiring book, I don't know what half those words mean! Reginald is a walking, talking, leaking word faucet. And he talks exactly the same in class as he talks during lunch. I know this kid, and I can tell you that he even uses big words and talks about insects and fossils when he's talking to his nine-month-old sister! He sounds like some kind of genius wizard all the time—whether he's with really little kids, his grandmother, guys at their lockers, his baby sister, or his soccer coach. He sounds like a grown-up, like some kind of professor, and he never turns it off so he can talk the plain old, ordinary, natural way most of us talk to each other at our not-so-great-to-be age. I bet his parents, aunts, uncles, and other grown-ups think that the way he talks is just fantastic. They worship their little professor. They are so proud of his amazing mind and mouth. But kids think he's strange because he can never switch to talking like a plain old normal, average kid. It's too bad; he's a very decent person with a bad reputation. Nobody really understands him; they think he's just trying to act smarter than they are and show them up. But I understand him. I don't think that's what Reginald's doing. He'd love to have friends, but let me tell you, this kid can't use slang. When he tries to say words like *cool* or *awesome,* they come out all wrong. He sounds even worse than he does when he gives you one of his lectures. Poor guy. I'd like to be friends with him myself, but even I, patient and kind Jarvis, get really sick to my stomach and tired of hearing him go on and on all the time. He keeps picking exactly the wrong things to talk about, and he talks about them for too long. And it's not always insects. He has a long list of carefully selected topics guaranteed to put you right to sleep—like asteroids, fossils, solar energy cells, and what he keeps calling *alternative fuels.* The first time I heard that expression, I thought he said alternative *fools,* and I thought he was talking about himself. But let's let good old reliable Dr. Levine say a few words about all these big words.

• MORE COMMENTS FROM DR. LEVINE ABOUT SOCIAL LANGUAGE •

As usual, Jarvis has made a big discovery. The truth is that Reginald has a problem with a very important part of social language called *code switching.* Social language uses special codes. We all need to speak several different codes, because we use different codes to talk to different people. When Reginald is in science class talking about paleontology, he's using just the right language code for that time and place. And maybe his parents and other relatives like to hear his scientific discussions. But other kids at lunch don't want to hear all that. Reginald needs to switch to a different language code, and use a kid code when he's with other students. We all know that there are times when you have to sound very polite and other times when that's not so necessary. You speak differently to someone you know really well than you do to someone you just met five minutes ago. You don't talk the same way to your dog as you talk to your uncle. You need to pick the right codes. Some people are great at code switching. They fit their words and sentences to the people they're with. Others, like Reginald, only talk in one code—the same code all the time. Often that code doesn't work; it might feel right, but it doesn't come out sounding right. Jarvis has learned something about this from his spying.

• • •

CODE SWITCHING

Code switching is a very important part of talking right. As you can see, you speak different ways depending upon whom you are with. Some students are much better at switching codes than others. When people use the wrong code for the people they're with, they sound strange and out of place.

Talking to a Teacher

Talking to a Baby

Talking to Parents

Talking to a Police Officer

Talking to Your Best Friend

Talking to a Pet

Talking to a Stranger

Talking to Your Little Sister

DIFFERENT CODES FOR DIFFERENT KIDS

Hi reader, time to wake up and drink your juice—it's Jarvis again. Let me tell you something Dr. Levine doesn't know that we kids mostly realize, even if we never talk or think about it. The thing is, you don't just switch codes when you go from talking to grown-ups to talking to kids, or from talking to a person to having a serious talk with your cousin's hermit crab. You also have to keep switching codes depending upon which kids you're talking to. You talk a little differently to kids you don't know too well or ones you want to get to be friends with than you do to kids who are already your very good friends. You use different words and stuff. Also, different groups of kids talk a little differently. You might need to learn to speak different kid-languages, which are different from the ones your group talks in.

A big part of code switching is talking like a kid when you're a still a kid, especially when you're with other kids. (By the way, it bugs me when adults try to talk like kids so that kids will think they're cool and just like them, but that's another story. Someday I'll write a book about immature grown-ups—there are plenty of those to spy on.) Anyway, it seems to me that some kids have trouble talking like kids. They can't use our ridiculous, colorful, crude kid-speak. Dr. Levine tells me that there are words that mainly kids use and that these words keep on changing over the years. He calls these words *lingo*, but I call them *slang*. Most of these words are perfectly clean and acceptable to parents, but some of them are what they call *dirty*. You take your chances with those, which mostly have less than five letters. Some kids are great at using all of these words. Other kids just can't use kid-talk in a way that sounds honest and right for them. They sound like they're doing a very bad job of imitating us slang-talking types. Guess who can't talk our talk? Reginald. He's a perfect example. Every once in a while, I notice him trying to use a kid word, and he gets it all wrong. It doesn't make sense and he uses the wrong kind of voice for it. Some kids have poor slang skills, I guess. Then there are some who talk too young, almost like baby talk, but we don't have a lot of those here at macho Eastern Middle School. I have to say that I, Jarvis, can flip the code switching switch and talk the talk, but I don't like to over-do it when I'm with a crowd of kids. That's definitely one of my social strengths.

So, Levine is mostly right: kids have to do a lot of that thing he calls code switching if they want to talk right. But he may not realize how often kids need to switch codes when they're together with other students. Let's not confuse him; he's a good guy. He just doesn't completely understand what middle school is like.

COMPLIMENTING SKILL

Now it's time for me to tell you something I realized one day while I was very busy taking very few notes for this very excellent book that Dr. Levine tricked me into writing with him. I was in our school library, which is this ancient room that has thousands of books that no living human being or domesticated animal has ever or would ever read. Whenever you're in there, you get stared at by this librarian person while you pretend to search for a very important book that you actually don't care if you find. Anyway, there I was, making believe that I was some kind of library genius looking something up when this really nice kid, Daniel, came up to me. We started talking very softly, so that our librarian (who was obviously trained to spy on students who like to talk a lot) wouldn't hear us. Daniel told me that that he really liked the comical story that I had written for English class that morning, and that he thought I was the funniest kid with the number one best sense of humor of anyone in the school.

First of all, I had to agree 100 percent with Daniel. I am the funniest kid I know! But also, believe me, what he said made me feel absolutely incredibly fantastic—to be told I was the best at something. And since I had been so busy with my social spying and social cognition, I realized all of a sudden that complimenting other people, saying things that help them feel good about themselves, is a very huge part of talking right. Then I began to notice that some of the most popular kids and those who had close friends were top-notch complimenters. And, wouldn't you know it, lots of my fellow students with a serious friend shortage never, ever—I mean not ever at all—gave anyone a compliment—except maybe themselves! It's as if they didn't know how to get compliment words out of their mouths. Wow! What a huge Jarvis espionage discovery: complimenting is a biggie in the world of talking right. You've gotta use up some words that make other people feel good pretty often. And you know, I'm not talking about phony compliments. I'm talking about the ones that you really mean. Maybe everybody should ask them-selves, "When's the last time I complimented somebody (and, of course, really meant it)?"

ASKING FOR THINGS: REQUESTING SKILL

Now I'm going to change the subject and talk about three other social language traps that I discovered that wipe out some kids in this school. One of them has to do with knowing how to ask for things without making other people hate and resent you. There's this girl named Cathy, and I have noticed that every time she wants something, she is just plain rude and crude in how she tries to get it. The other day, we were in art class, and there was not enough paint thinner to go around. All of a sudden, Cathy shouted, "I'm using the rest of that paint thinner." That made some kids really mad. I think she could have and should have said, "I'd like to use the rest of the paint thinner if that's OK." At lunch, she did the same thing and shouted, "Hurry up and move over so I can sit here." She said it like she was everybody's boss or something. Other kids didn't say anything, but you could tell that they were put off by the way she kept asking for things as if we were all supposed to be her servants or something. When I talked to Dr. Levine about what Cathy does, he said that her problem is called poor *requesting skills*—he's got some kind of name for everything, but that's *his* problem. He likes to show off his vocabulary. But if it will impress him and other adults, then you and I can try to start understanding and using those big social cognition words.

TRYING TO BE FUNNY: HUMOR REGULATION

Another thing I want to spend some serious time on is joking, on how kids try to be funny or why they think they're funny. Check out Jeff talking to some other seventh graders on the bus the other day:

Luis: We have to go to hockey practice so early tomorrow morning.

Tony: Yeah, at six o'clock, the coach said. It's the only time we can get on the ice.

·114·

Jeff: Hey, do you guys know why hockey's too expensive for some kids to play?

Luis: No, why?

Jeff: 'Cause it costs a lot of pucks. Get it?

[Jeff laughs and laughs, but no one else seems to think it's funny.]

Jeff: And here's another great one: why did the rocket ship land on the football field? You give up? So it could get a touchdown!

[Jeff can't stop laughing at his own joke. The other kids look at each other and don't even smile.]

Jeff: How about this one: why did the baseball player keep holding his nose? You give up? Because of all the foul balls!

[By this time, Jeff is laughing so hard that he can hardly talk, but the poor kid never even notices that he is the only one laughing at his jokes.]

It's not so cool to keep laughing at your own jokes, especially if you're the only one who thinks they're funny. Also, I wonder why Jeff never noticed that he was the only one laughing? If he had seen that, he might have decided to be serious for a while, but instead he kept telling more and more bad jokes that were about as funny as getting an injection. The other guys tried to ignore him. They probably wished they could jump out of that bus. I bet they didn't want to sit anywhere near him the next morning. And you know what else? Tony and Luis were trying to have a serious conversation about hockey, and Luis kept kidding around. I think that his social signal receiver should have picked up the serious talk of the other guys and tried to fit his talking in with it. Jeff didn't get it.

SHYNESS

My last thing on social talking has to do with a girl named Emily, who seems like a really good person but who is definitely in the Mostly Hidden category (see page 19 in case you forgot what that means). Nobody really knows Emily. That's because she almost never, ever says anything. When I turned on my recorder to catch her speaking, there was complete, total, 100 percent silence—like blank tape. That's because Emily is unbelievably shy. She hardly even looks at other people. I think she thinks that if she doesn't look at people, she won't have to talk to them. One of Emily's friends told me that Emily never ever calls anyone on the phone; it's like she's afraid to have a phone conversation. It's just the same in class. She's in my science class, and she never opens her mouth except sometimes to breathe. Come to think of it, she doesn't do that much either. Maybe she has gills like a goldfish. When Mr. Benson calls on her, she answers so quietly that you can hardly hear her. But you know what? I heard that Emily is a real brain; she gets As in everything. And it's not that she has no friends at all. There are a couple of girls she hangs around with sometimes—nobody knows them too well either.

By the way, I have to tell you that there are other kids, both boys and girls, who are kind of like Emily. I mean, they don't say much. But we also have a ton of kids here at Eastern Middle School who talk too much. They can't stop talking, even when they have nothing to say. Their mouths are on automatic pilot. And often their volume switch is turned up too loud. Words just keep blowing and howling out of their mouths like tornadoes all the time, non-stop. They can be totally annoying to everyone. So, reader, some kids talk too little, others talk too much, and most of us probably talk just the right amount. But your friend Jarvis is now talking more than he should. So let's turn things over to good Dr. Mel, who might want to talk more about talking more—or less.

• FINAL COMMENTS FROM DR. LEVINE ABOUT SOCIAL LANGUAGE •

Jarvis has come up with more good insights about the language side of getting along with people. We now have more ingredients for talking right. First, we had the example of Reginald. The poor kid has two problems. He has trouble choosing the right topics, and he has trouble talking about them for the right length of time. Reginald kept going on and on about paleontology, which just doesn't fit well during a relaxing lunch break with kids who have no special interest in fossils. Also, he just kept going on without stopping. So we can say that Reginald has a problem with *topic selection* and *length.* That really puts people off—especially when it happens often, which sadly is the case with Reginald. Almost every day he picks things to talk about that other people aren't interested in, and he has trouble stopping. Also, he doesn't seem to notice when other people are getting bored or annoyed.

Reginald has another social language problem: he talks almost exactly the same way to everyone at all times. A good social speaker knows that the way you talk with your sister is different from the way you talk to your mom and the way you talk to a new teacher or a complete stranger you meet in the dentist's waiting room. Poor Reginald talks his very grown-up professor-speak wherever he goes and with everyone. He doesn't seem to realize that talk like that works very well in the classroom and when you're showing your relatives how smart you are, but it really bugs other students. He needs to change to kid talk when he's with kids. But Reginald is stuck; he can't switch his language code to fit with the people he's with.

Jarvis hit on something very important in the school library when Daniel complimented him for his excellent sense of humor. Everybody loves to receive compliments. Compliments are great for our self-esteem. And Jarvis was right on target when he realized that the ability to give compliments, your *complimenting skill,* is a major part of talking right. For some people, giving compliments is very natural; others have to work on building their complimenting skills, which can then help them build friendships. Of course, as Jarvis pointed out, compliments have to be sincere, not fake. But it is possible to find something to compliment in everyone. We're not saying you have to keep complimenting people all day long, but every so often, compliments can make relationships much stronger and closer.

Jarvis also introduced us to Cathy, the girl who has trouble asking for things without irritating everyone around her. As I said before, she has poor *requesting skills.* There's no doubt about it: how you ask for something influences whether you're going to get what you want. And how you make requests can also affect how other people feel about you. No one likes or respects someone who acts as if everyone owes him or her something. That kind of attitude is arrogant—it makes you seem as if you feel superior to everyone else. That's no way to get others to like you!

Humor is a big issue. Everybody likes kids who know how to be funny. But being humorous is tricky. Nothing's worse than trying to say funny things that only you think are funny. That's what we saw in Jeff, who was a very unsuccessful comedian. Only he laughed at his jokes. Being socially good with humor isn't always so easy. You need to know when to try to be funny (and when it's better to be serious), how to be funny (different people have different ways they can be funny), what kind of humor to use (depending on the people you're with), and when it's time to stop kidding around. We call all of that *humor regulation.* Of course, when you're having lots of trouble regulating humor, you might be better off being serious!

HOW MUCH AND HOW LOUD YOU TALK

How much you talk is another big issue Jarvis brought up. Emily is an extremely shy girl who never says very much. We don't know why she is so quiet. Some people seem to be born shy—it's just their temperament or personality. Some kids become shy because they have had their feelings hurt too often. Shyness sometimes occurs when people have trouble expressing themselves, when they can't get their ideas into words and sentences quickly and accurately enough. We say that people with those difficulties have *expressive language* problems. Also, some students act shy because they don't have enough confidence in themselves. They feel inferior to other kids, even though they shouldn't feel that way.

By the way, as Jarvis observed, we come across many people who talk too much. They seem to have little, if any, control over their mouths, which seem to be in constant motion. These students sometimes get in trouble for the things they say. They just blurt out whatever's on their mind, and sometimes they say things they shouldn't say, things that are rude, dirty, cruel, or completely silly. There are lots of things we think about that we should never say. Fortunately, most of us have an editor working in our brains, deciding what we should say out loud and what we should keep inside.

One more thing to think about is the how loud someone talks. There are some people who have trouble controlling their voice volume. They shout when they don't need to. Everyone can hear what they're saying, even across the room, which is only OK if they're saying something interesting. Most of the time talking too loud is a social problem. It can seriously bother other people.

SELF-MONITORING

One final point before I let Jarvis wind up this chapter: many of the kids he spied on for this chapter have one major thing in common. They don't realize how the way they talk affects other people. They never get the feedback. They don't watch peoples' facial expressions or body movements to pick up their reactions. It's crucial to always be aware of how you're doing socially while you are with other people. It's also important to be able to think back over recent social experiences and try to decide how well you performed. Did you talk right? Or did you say some things you wish you hadn't said? How could you have done better with the way you spoke—your topic selection, code switching, conversational skill, and the other parts of social language that we have looked at in this chapter. If the students in this chapter had been more aware of how they were speaking, they could have changed the way they were talking or altered what they were talking about. They just didn't know how they were doing because they were not using the social self-monitoring skills that we talked about in Chapter 1. That's too bad, because those skills are crucial. Fortunately, when you find you have a part of social cognition that's weak, you can work on improving it—partially just by thinking about it while you're with other people.

In the box on the next page, I have summarized the social language parts that we have covered in this chapter:

EXPRESSING THE RIGHT FEELINGS

CONVERSATIONAL SKILL

CONTROL OF BOASTING

LISTENING

CODE SWITCHING

TOPIC SELECTION AND LENGTH

COMPLIMENTING SKILL

REQUESTING SKILL

HUMOR REGULATION

SHYNESS

LANGUAGE OUTPUT: AMOUNT & VOLUME LEVEL

SOCIAL LANGUAGE SELF-MONITORING

It's Jarvis here to wrap up this chapter. OK readers, we have now learned how to talk right, or at least how not to talk wrong when we're with other people which is, of course, when we do most of our talking—hopefully. With my recordings, overhearings, and observations and Levine's partly interesting comments, it is easy to see how much language helps or hurts our social lives. What you say and how you say it can make or break you when it comes to getting along. Even what you don't say can hurt you, but you don't have to worry about how you say what you don't say! So we all need to think hard about talking. To help us deal with this awesome responsibility, Dr. Levine, for a very large additional fee, will now provide some incredibly simple questions for discussion in your class, or you can answer them with yourself in front of a mirror, or you can make believe that your book doesn't have the next page in it. You could even ignore all the questions and skip to the superinteresting Jarvis projects. After the questions, we will be allowed to move along to the next thrilling chilling chapter of *Jarvis Clutch—Social Spy,* a chapter which will tell you much more than you want to know about acting right in the social universe.

SOME SOCIAL QUESTIONS AND PROJECTS FROM THIS CHAPTER TO THINK ABOUT, DO, AND/OR DISCUSS

1. A kid is always boasting and bragging. He or she can't stop talking about himself or herself. He or she never seems to say anything positive about anybody else. Is that a social language problem? If he or she were your neighbor, would you say something about it to him or her? If so, how would you say it?

2. List the different language codes that you think you speak (such as kid talk, dog talk, baby talk, etc.). What are the different kinds of people (or animals!) for whom you have to change the way talk?

3. How important is it to talk the current lingo that most kids use in your community? Are there certain words that popular kids use? What are some examples of important words that are now used a lot in your school? Do kids who never use these terms have social problems?

4. What's meant by a "good sense of humor"? What things would a person with a "terrible sense of humor" be doing wrong?

5. Can you give any examples of times when you've had trouble knowing what to talk about with someone? What did you do in that situation?

6. If someone described you as "a really great conversationalist," what are some things you would be doing right during conversations?

7. What are some common social language mistakes that you have heard kids make?

8. Can you think of any kids you know who you think have excellent social language? What is it about they way they talk that helps them make friends and be liked by others?

9. What can you do if you've just made a social language mistake and you realize it?

10. How can kids improve their social language?

11. Are there some parts of talking right that Jarvis or Dr. Levine mention that don't really matter at your school? What are they? Are there some aspects of talking right that were not mentioned in this chapter and yet are important at your school? What are they?

★ JARVIS PROJECTS FOR CHAPTER 4 ★

Writing Project: Write a conversation between two kids who have social language problems. Make a recording of your conversation, or act it out with one of your classmates. Choose one of the following social language problems to write about in your dialogue (or add your own topic if that's what you like to do):

• Someone with a topic selection problem
• A kid showing poor conversation abilities
• A student who boasts or brags too much and never praises anyone else
• A boy or girl who says things in a way that sounds mean (even though he or she doesn't mean to)
• Someone who uses humor the wrong way
• Someone who doesn't know how to ask for things or share
• A kid who doesn't use the right language code with a new friend
• A kid who doesn't use the right language code with a teacher or other adult

Think about what your dialogue would sound like if the kids in it had really fantastic social language skills. Rewrite your conversation, and fix the social language problems.

Spy Mission: Spend a day keeping your eyes and ears open for social language problems on the bus, in the hallway, in class, in the cafeteria, and after school. When you hear someone talking with a social language problem, take a few notes. At the end of the day, write a few sentences about how each problem could be solved.

~ CHAPTER 5 ~
ACTING RIGHT

And now, ladies and gentlemen, here once again is Jarvis Clutch to entertain, inform, inspire, and impress his fascinated audience. In the last chapter of *Jarvis Clutch—Social Spy* (remember that one?), Levine and I talked about talking, about how what you say and how you say it show the world a lot about your social cognition, all that special brain wiring that helps you become a social success (if that's what you want). We decided that you can really blow it socially if you don't talk right. But guess what? Even if you do know how to talk social talk, you haven't got it completely made. No way! You see, you also have to act right! You can't just say the right things; you're also supposed to *do* the right things. Some folks are never satisfied! To find out more about what works and what doesn't when it comes to how you act, your top-secret investigator Jarvis opened his droopy eyelids as far as they can go and wandered around school checking on how kids were acting with each other. Once again, I mostly spied on the kids who acted wrong, at least wrong if they cared about other kids liking them and wanting to be with them.

AGGRESSION AVOIDANCE

During one of our way-too-long meetings to discuss this way-too-long book, Dr. Levine told me something that was almost interesting. He mentioned that some teenagers with social cognition problems are very aggressive or pushy, and others are passive or sort of timid. He asked me if I could think of any-one in my class who fit in the aggressive category. I thought about it really hard for nearly two seconds until the Bomber flew in and bombarded my brain. This guy's real name is Palmer, but everyone calls him the Bomber because he is so aggressive. Wherever he goes, he drops bombs that cause social explosions. And you know, he always bombs out with other kids. (Isn't that clever? I thought of that one myself.) I don't think you really know what the word *aggressive* means until you've had a chance to watch someone like the Bomber in action at Eastern Middle School. So, that's what Jarvis Clutch, Social Spy did. I watched the Bomber do his thing.

For three days, I secretly followed Palmer the Bomber through the halls, in the lunchroom, and around other historic battlefields at our battling school. Of course, I'm such a slick, sly spy that the Bomber didn't know he was being trailed. The first morning, the school's screechy, creepy buzzer sounded off at 9:10, signaling the start of my Bomber espionage assignment. (By the way, we have specially designed torture chamber buzzer bells at Eastern that wake you up at the end of each period, but wreck your eardrums so that you can't listen to anything in your next class. It's even hard to go back to sleep…only kidding.) But back to the Bomber. As soon as the door of his class swung open, the Bomber took off with his supersonic jet engines revved up as high as they could go. I found out that he always has to be the first one through any doorway. He zoomed through the runways of the school blasting through everything and everyone in his way. He always acted as if he was trying to run for some kind of game-winning touchdown. He would collide with other kids and never say that he was sorry. During my three days of spying on him, I saw him wipe out at least twenty-five innocent bystanders to get to his locker or to enjoy a drink of the very warm, rusty, totally polluted liquid in our two very popular drinking fountains (it's really sickening because the water pressure is so low you get to taste the metal part with your tongue and lips and catch everybody's deadly germs when you try to get a drink). At lunch, the Bomber had to be the first in line no matter how much aggressive pushing and shoving it took. It was as if he was competing with everybody all the time. He had to be number one, but number one what? It didn't make any sense, no sense at all. Along the way, the Bomber got into fights pretty often. He is huge for a person our age—tall, and loaded with heavy fat or muscle or very thick skin, I can't be sure. So, he could hurt someone, and sometimes he really does. But he never says that he is sorry. And you know, it isn't as if he wants to destroy anyone. Maybe he doesn't realize how strong he is. He acts as if it is just natural to be aggressive and act tough all the time. To tell you the truth, this kid has the personality of a tarantula. In fact, I've met some tarantulas with much better social cognition than the Bomber!

I am 200 percent sure that the Bomber doesn't have the least tiny, microscopic speck of an idea of how he comes across to everybody else. Otherwise, he would act differently. He has a horrible reputation. Nobody can stand the Bomber, but he acts as if being the bad guy is so natural for him. He spends a lot of hours outside the assistant principal's office reading the three-year-old, torn-up copy of *Outdoor Life* that Mr. Jensen very generously donated to our school two-and-a-half years ago. It seems that the Bomber is always in hot water. But more than anything else, the Bomber is just plain inconsiderate. He never seems to ask himself the million-dollar social cognition question: "How would I feel if someone did that to me?" He doesn't seem to think about anyone but himself. Even when he tries to be friendly, which is some of the time, he acts tough, too tough, and too physical. He slaps kids hard on the back or punches them in the stomach in a very friendly way that makes it hard for them to breathe.

After three days of spying on the Bomber, I followed him into the lunchroom—I got to be second in line that way—and I sat down next to him. You'd think he had really smelly, totally foul skunk breath since nobody ever sits next to this kid unless it is the last seat in the room. Never let it be said that your one and only favorite social spy is a coward; I was actually totally scared out of my little old mind, but I decided that this was a time to be brave, to tough it out. And it worked out for me. The Bomber and I talked about a lot of things. I asked him whether he likes being one of the strongest and biggest kids in his class. At first he didn't say anything. Then he said, "It's OK, but sometimes when kids are scared of you, they don't like you much." Then I told him that it wasn't fair that other students often said such rotten things about him. I said that they never talk about any of the good things that he does or says. Like they never mention the fact that he is really good with computers and that he's willing to help anybody anytime who's got a computer glitch. They never talk about how great he is on a skateboard. The Bomber then said something that was like an electric shock for this Social Spy. He told me, "I don't blame them. Sometimes I don't even like myself very much. Jarvis, I'm starting to think that I just can't act right with other kids. It's like I just don't know how to do it. Everything that feels OK to me in the way I behave everyone else can't stand. I've been told I'm much too aggressive. To me, it doesn't feel that way. I'm just being myself. And that means it seems really natural to be competing with everyone and pushing them around all the time, not like competing in sports or on tests, but in everything else. It's kinda how I'm wired, but now I know it's not working right for me. I used to think it was cool to be called Palmer the Bomber, but now it sounds to me like I'm some kind of freak. I just don't know how to change. Look, yesterday was my fourteenth birthday. Maybe it's too late to change." I stared at this gigantic jet powered machine and noticed that his brown eyes were swimming around in water. Yes, this big lug looked as if he was trying hard not to cry.

Anyway, your tough Social Spy, good old Jarvis, decided that the Bomber needed to go back to the hangar for some serious fixing up, not from your local aircraft repair shop but from someone who really knows something about those very complicated things called teenagers. So, after my three days of spying on the Bomber, I visited Mr. Ramirez, a really good guy who I think definitely understands us. He is called a school adjustment counselor or something like that. By the way, with that name, I think he should also be spending time adjusting the school—Eastern could use some repairs. I told

Mr. Ramirez about my conversation with Palmer, which I decided to call him from then on. Mr. Ramirez was very impressed with me, or at least that's what he told me. Of course, he knew Palmer (much too well), which meant that he was no fan of his, so he was extra glad that I had spent some time talking with Palmer. I told Mr. Ramirez that I thought that it was like Palmer was socially blind and could never see how the way he acted turned everybody against him. Palmer thought that being tough would make all of the other kids respect him or something. I told Mr. Ramirez that I was really worried about Palmer, that he seemed very, very sad, and that I didn't want him to try to kill himself. Mr. Ramirez said that since Palmer had talked to me like that, he was probably ready to start working on his social cognition. He thought that Palmer probably just didn't know any other way to act around kids, and that he needed to learn some new social skills. Mr. Ramirez thanked me and said that he would set up a meeting with Palmer. He started to see Palmer and teach him about social cognition. Then Palmer got to be part of what they call a social skills group; it's like a small club of kids with social cognition problems that get together and try to improve. Guess what? I think he's doing much better—a whole lot. Palmer was completely wrong about one thing—it's never too late to change. I have decided that social cognition comes totally naturally to some kids, but others, like Palmer, have to be taught the subject, like it's math or a foreign language. Who knows? Maybe I saved his life, or at least his reputation.

I guess everybody feels like being aggressive sometimes. Maybe there's somebody you are mad at or feel jealous of, and there might be a part of you that wants to hurt that person or push him or her around, either physically or in some other way. Let's say there's some kid who seems really stuck-up and owns a lot of stuff you can't afford, and his parents drive a really expensive car that you wish your family could buy. This can make you mad (and jealous!) even though it shouldn't. Then, if you get a chance to be mean to that kid, say by taking two cups of fruit punch in the lunchroom and using up the last of it so he or she can't get any, you might do it to get back at him or her. Or when this kid isn't looking, you might hide his or her finished homework so that he or she gets in trouble for not handing it in. You never knew Jarvis could think up such totally mean thoughts did you? I bet every kid gets tempted to do these kind of mean things, but most of them realize that their aggressive plans would be really stupid, so they don't go through with them. Congratulations! Even your very kind, sweet, gentle, nice guy Jarvis feels that way sometimes. But these feelings can get out of hand and get you into big, big trouble. So how do you cool it? How do you put out the fires inside of you? Dr Levine calls that *aggression avoidance*. Boy, does he like those big words that he thinks he can impress us with! Let's find out what he means by this.

• DR. LEVINE'S THOUGHTS ABOUT AGGRESSION AVOIDANCE •

There are many kids who have social problems because they are too aggressive. These kids have trouble with *aggression avoidance.* There's some aggression inside of everyone. We all feel aggressive and very angry at times, but we try to work out our frustration so that things don't get worse. Most people want to avoid aggression even when they feel very angry, and most of us can stop ourselves from doing things that are violent. However, people with aggression avoidance problems don't control this feeling. They often get into trouble without even realizing that they are getting themselves into trouble until it is too late. Very aggressive students are not usually well-liked by most other kids, and their teachers and parents obviously aren't too pleased with them either. And as Jarvis found out, sometimes aggressive kids are not too happy inside themselves.

• • •

When kids act too rough, tough, or aggressive with other people, there are always good reasons for it. These reasons are often misunderstood. In fact, most of the time even aggressive people don't even know why they are behaving in that way! It's usually not their fault. This diagram shows some of the common reasons for aggressive behavior.

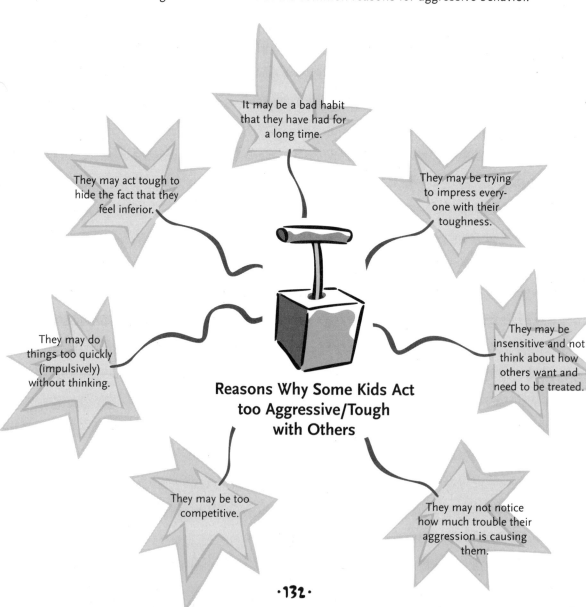

It may be a bad habit that they have had for a long time.

They may act tough to hide the fact that they feel inferior.

They may be trying to impress everyone with their toughness.

They may do things too quickly (impulsively) without thinking.

They may be insensitive and not think about how others want and need to be treated.

Reasons Why Some Kids Act too Aggressive/Tough with Others

They may be too competitive.

They may not notice how much trouble their aggression is causing them.

Different things can cause kids to be aggressive. Some aggressive kids are just very impulsive; they do bad things too fast without thinking about them. I think Palmer (the Bomber) showed some of this. Impulsive kids get in trouble even though they didn't really intend to cause trouble. Other students just don't seem to know how to act right with other kids. They only think about themselves and don't really understand that they are turning everyone off by acting the way they do. That's also a problem for Palmer. He doesn't have the social cognition to act right with other people. He doesn't realize the effect that he has on his classmates. When he's mean to them, he doesn't notice the expressions on their faces. He doesn't seem to read the feedback that could let him know that he's making enemies and getting a really terrible reputation. Poor kid. He acts tough but he feels sad. It's also true that acting a certain way all the time can get to be a habit that can be very hard to break. You can see that happening with Palmer. He got his reputation as a bomber and somehow that stuck. He even started to think of himself as a kind of a bomber—so he just keeps bombing away! People expect him to be a troublemaker, and he expects to be one too. So, he plays the role, almost like an actor in a movie. I'm very glad Palmer is getting help with this. Mr. Ramirez will probably spend time explaining more to him about his bad reputation, getting him to think about ways to avoid being aggressive, teaching him to watch for the effect he's having on other students, and figuring out some ways to act, ways that don't wreck his reputation and get him into social trouble.

SOCIAL REACTING

OK, OK, once again Levine taught us something we already knew: how you act can mess up or build up your social life. Nobody much likes people who act evil or mean around everybody—except maybe the buddies who help them act like some kind of demon. But in my spy travels around Eastern Middle School this year, I have made another revolutionary Jarvis discovery, which is that it's not just how you act that counts. How you *react* is just as crucial. Let me tell how I found that out.

There's this girl who has no friends, at least none that I could find anywhere. Maybe she keeps them hidden in places that are off-limits even to a clever spy like Jarvis. One day I was watching Fiona put things in her locker. Fiona is the tiniest girl in her class. She's almost invisible, she's so small. She moves fast, kind of buzzing around like a mosquito. Getting back to the locker scene, two girls were standing near Fiona, and one of them called her a very bad word that the publisher will not permit me to include on this page, even though it kills and I would give anything to tell you, my reader, what that word was. I'm sure you have heard it before. Anyway, this girl called Fiona that name and then attacked with other very cruel comments about her height. Then, all of a sudden, like a satellite blasting off from its launch pad, Fiona let loose with her own explosion of the world's most powerful curse words, along with some crafty insults about one of the girl's pimples and the other's stubby fingers and some other body parts I am not permitted to mention on these pages. It was as gross as it gets. I tried not to, but I had to laugh (not good technique for a seasoned spy). I didn't think Fiona had it in her. In a way, I kind of enjoyed seeing her stand up to those girls. But then the other two girls fired back at Fiona with more horrible insults and were soon joined by two more of their shouting friends. They all seemed to be having a ball setting Fiona off like a hand grenade. Pretty soon Fiona just walked away, practically in tears. Here's the question I wondered about and the one I want you, the reader of this fascinating book, to wonder about too:

did Fiona handle this well? Did she *react* right to the very mean insults from those attacking girls in her class? What else could she have done?

OK, here are a few Jarvis choices. You can tell me which one you like best:

    a. Fiona could have kicked one of the girls or bashed some heads with her science book.

    b. She could have ignored them completely.

    c. She could have just cried and cried and made them feel really guilty.

    d. She could have tried changing the subject or saying something nice to one of the girls to change the mood of everything.

    e. She could have made a little joke and quietly walked away.

    f. She shouldn't have done any of the above—there are better ways to react.

Would you like to know what I think? Of course you would. I would react to this bad situation by trying either *d* or *e* or maybe a little of each. I don't know what Dr. Levine would advise. What would you do, socially skilled reader, if you were Fiona? Personally, I believe Fiona has a real social cognition weakness; she can't control they way she reacts to things, and the way she reacts to things makes her extremely unpopular. I bet that Levine has a few things to say about this. I will call on him now, especially since he will jump in even if I don't call on him.

• DR. LEVINE'S COMMENTS ON SOCIAL REACTING •

Jarvis has now shown us the importance of acting and reacting right in the social world. Both of these abilities take a lot of good judgment, and they take time. Some kids get into difficulties with others because they don't really stop and think before they act or react. Others do slow down and find the best ways to act and react. Still others, even when they think hard about it, have trouble acting and reacting without angering or turning off their classmates. They have to find an adult who can teach them about making good decisions about what to do in the social world. By the way, like Jarvis I would also choose *d* or *e*. I would have trouble ignoring the situation completely. But, of course, different people have different ways of reacting.

FOUR BIG *C*s: CONFLICT REPAIR, CONTROL, COLLABORATION, AND COMPETITION

To change the subject just a little, I noticed something when Jarvis provided me with the information he had picked up during his social spy missions at Eastern Middle School. I noticed that he had come across four crucial parts of social cognition, and that they all began with the letter *C*. They are: conflict repair, collaboration, competitive behavior, and control. The best way to understand their importance is to see how they work or don't work by looking at examples provided by Jarvis, our observant spy.

CONFLICT REPAIR

At Eastern Middle School, some kid gets into an argument approximately every four seconds (that's on a good day). I see students disagreeing or fighting over something wherever I go. That probably happens at every joyous school—even *your* peace-loving place of learning. I know that most kids I see around here have serious differences of opinion, fights, or red-hot arguments, sometimes even with their best friends. So, the big question is not whether or not you have run-ins with other kids. The big deal is how good you are at fixing the damage, straightening out the glitches, bouncing back, and solving the problems that caused the war. Here is an example from my excellent spy notes.

There are these two girls who are in the eighth grade like me, but they don't really know me. Their names are Uma and Aretha—or something like that. Anyway, these two are together all the time. When you see one, you know you're gonna spot the other one a few feet away. It's like invisible wires attach them to each other. Anyway, a few weeks ago, I was doing my heavy-duty spy work while everyone was waiting to get on the bus after school. These two girls looked really angry with each other. Their noses were wrinkled up and they were showing their fangs like two fuming dogs about to square off. I turned up the volume on my right ear (the one that does the best spy work) and found out that a girl named Caroline had invited Aretha to come to her house and watch a video and have pizza on Friday night, and then stay over for a slumber party with three other girls (sounds totally dumb to me). The problem is that Caroline hadn't invited Uma, who said she wouldn't go any-way because Caroline is such an "lame-o."

To get on with this fabulous suspense-thriller story, Uma told Aretha that they could no longer be friends if Aretha went to the party, and that she would never, ever even talk to Aretha again for both of their whole lives (or whichever one ends first, I guess). What a crisis! The headline would read: "Two Friends Declare War in a Vicious Social Dispute." I bet Aretha wanted to go to that party really badly. You see, Aretha had to feel proud that she got that invitation, and you can be sure that Uma was badly insulted that she wasn't invited. Her feelings were probably about as hurt as feelings get. Uma had been almost fatally wounded in the Eastern Middle School social battle-ground. It had to be especially hard since Uma thought that Caroline was her friend. Our early teenage lives are complicated, aren't they, reader? Maybe Uma was a little bit jealous of her friend Aretha. Sometimes even the best of friends, the closest kids, especially those attached by invisible wires, kind of compete with each other and can get jealous of each other really easily—at least that's what I've noticed here at good old uptight Eastern Middle School. Close friends can sometimes be almost as vicious as brothers and sisters or hammerhead sharks.

Well, the buses were late leaving that afternoon, so I got a good chance to spy on these two girls. Here's what I found out: Aretha was great at handling the conflict, and Uma was useless. Uma kept saying, "I hate you" and looking totally sad (even crying a little) and burning up with anger at Aretha. "This is the end of our friendship. I can't stand you anymore, Aretha! All you care about is yourself, not me, not anyone else. You're the most selfish person I ever met. You can disappear as far as I'm concerned. And I don't care." She also used a few other words I'm not allowed to include in this book because it may be used in some schools where they censor what kids read. But then, like magic, Aretha came to the rescue and was like a social genius in fixing things up and making peace. She said, "Uma, why don't I tell Caroline that I don't feel like going to her house unless you're invited too. Or else, I'll just go there for a few minutes and I won't even sleep over. I'll tell them that I can't stay over because I need to go somewhere with my friend Uma. Then maybe they'll want both of us there. Besides, it would be more fun for me if you were with me." Wow! The Aretha magic touch. Aretha the Social Superstar really knew how to bandage up the conflict, but her friend Uma

was a disaster when it came to social repair work. Uma had no idea what to do when there was an argument or disagreement; she just made it worse and worse. It's kinda like Uma poured grease on the fire and Aretha squirted water on it. Maybe that's why so many kids really like Aretha and think she's easy to get along with, and hardly anyone wants to be friends with Uma. But Aretha is able to see Uma's good side, and they really like each other. It's possible that what Aretha did is what Levine means by *conflict repair*. Why does he always use those big words? Why does Levine think the only way to get people to like him or admire him is by teaching them those kinds of words? Well, that's his problem. I'm hoping he'll pick up a few social tips from this book.

SOCIAL CONTROL

Dr. Levine says that what I'm going to talk about next is called *social control*, number two on his list of four big Cs. I've got a good example of control. There's this group of about twelve kids that hang around together most of the time. On weekends, you see them having lunch together, and in school they swarm together like hornets (and they sometimes sting other kids). There are boys and girls in the group, and they all play a lot of sports. Your master Social Spy, none other than Jarvis Clutch, inconspicuously followed this crowd around to see how they act together, and I found out something pretty amazing. Different members of the group have different amounts of influence within the group.

TOO MUCH SOCIAL CONTROL

There's this one kid Allen, who makes everyone do the things he wants to do whenever he wants to do them, even if the others don't feel like it. Get that? He tries to be the boss of everything, and most of the time he is. But sometimes the others get really annoyed at Allen and resent him. They refuse to do something his way. Then old Allen just splits; he takes off by himself. He won't be part of the group unless he can control everyone and everything. He's basically an OK guy. He has a likable personality, is good-looking (in a phony kind of way, at least in your spy's opinion), and is respected for his sports ability and brains. Most of the time everyone lets him have his way, and they seem to follow him like he's at the head of a flock of geese flying in V formation. But I wonder what he's going to do someday when he finds himself with people who want to be his friends without having to follow his lead. Can Allen ever be friends with people without controlling them?

NOT ENOUGH SOCIAL CONTROL

Then there are two kids in the group who are just the opposite of Allen. They have no control, no power at all, or at least they've given up all their control over how they act when they're with the group. Patti and Mark are the world's wimpiest followers. They talk like everyone else, dress like everyone else, and do what everyone else wants to do—even if they don't really want to do it. They don't have any control. Let me tell you, sleepy reader, these two had a big problem two weeks ago when they were at David's house with their group. David's an important member of their gang. It was late in the afternoon, and both of his parents were still at work. The whole gang was watching some very bad movie or playing video games and talking about kids in school they can't stand. Then someone said that he was thirsty. David opened a cabinet to see if he could find some soda. His friends saw some beer and whiskey in the cabinet and quickly grabbed it. David, a nice guy with only a small amount of control (more than Patti and Mark, but less than Allen), allowed the kids to try some of the drinks. Patti and Mark didn't really want to join in, but they did anyway. Guess who were the only kids to get caught? You got it—Patti and Mark. They drank too much, and their parents could smell it on their breath. They were grounded for two weeks, and everybody at school talked about them. Even their teachers found out. These poor kids with no social control got sucked in. They became like servants just trying to please other kids without thinking about what feels right for them.

I know some other kids like that at Eastern Middle School that don't have enough social control. They decide to quit playing the violin (even though they're good at it), stop studying for math (even if it's their favorite subject), or wear clothes they don't even like just to get accepted by other students. They give away all their control over themselves. I think that's what Dr. Levine and other adults who think they understand us adolescents call *peer pressure*. Remember that term from Chapter 2? By the way, adults don't understand as much as they think they do, but we shouldn't hurt their feelings—they're very sensitive when it comes to what they think they know about taking care of us. They can get really depressed and upset if you tell them they don't know what they're talking about. And besides, I bet adults have to handle peer pressure too. Anyway, sorry to change the subject, but this is super important. There's a whole lot of peer pressure around. Some kids handle it well and can still be themselves and have some freedom, but others give up everything. They stop being themselves. They lose their freedom. They just do whatever they need to do to get other kids to like and accept them. They have no more control! This is the problem that Patti and

Mark have. Others are in their driver's seat, like Allen. There must be a way of having just the right amount of control—not so much that you're a total loner and not so little that you're a social slave.

Speaking of control, there was one day after school when I spied on a bunch of seventh graders playing basketball. There was this one kid, Dimitri, who was a serious problem for his team. He kept hogging the ball, as if he were planning to eat it for lunch tomorrow. When he didn't have the ball, he kept shouting, "Gimme the ball! Gimme the ball! Pass it here!" Then, when Dimitri had the ball he wouldn't pass it to anyone else. You could tell he wanted to make all the baskets himself. Even when three guys were guarding him, he would still take shots. There was no way he could make them, but he took them anyway—and he missed every time. Then he would get really angry and accuse the other guys of fouling him. But, of course, there was no referee to agree with Dimitri or tell him to cool it. Dimitri, the big-shot hero. What a total jerk! Another kid came over to me and complained that Dimitri doesn't belong on a team, and that he should just play by himself all the time. You can't be a team player when you have to be in complete control all the time. Isn't that right, reader?

COLLABORATION

Your spy spied something similar one day in an art class. Six kids were working on a project. They were building these great pyramids, like the kind they have in Egypt. There was this one girl, Emily, who I have to admit is a very good artist. And boy did she let everyone else know it! She really took over and started bossing the other kids around. Kyle, who is definitely not known for his talent as a pyramid builder (his hands are mainly for show; they don't seem to do much), kinda messed up when he tried to make the base of one of the pyramids. It was so crooked that the whole pyramid was ready to fall over into the Nile River that was being made out of some thick, sticky goop dyed blue. Boy, did Emily let him have it! First, she insulted him in front of everyone, and then she went ahead and made the base herself without even explaining to Kyle how to do it. She acted as if she was the only one who knew what was going on. She was completely bossy, but Ms. Greenwelt never said that she was the boss. And you know, reader, Emily always tries to take over when she works with anyone, and she always wants all the credit from the teacher. Most of the time nobody wants to work with her. I have a funny feeling that Dr. Levine would say that Dimitri and Emily are kids who have trouble *collaborating*. That would be his usual complicated way of saying something pretty simple: they have problems working together with others.

COMPETITIVE BEHAVIOR

Now, all of this makes Jarvis, your favorite Social Spy, think about something else that we kids don't like to talk about too much. What I'm thinking about here is *competition,* trying to be better than other kids at everything we can. I know what you're thinking: speak for yourself, Jarvis. I think kids all want to be number one—but they can't. Not everyone can get an *A* on a book report, make the football team, or get invited to someone's party. There's always competition, and in the end, some people win and some people lose. You even compete with your best friends, at least some of the time. That can make things really tense. And you almost never stop competing with your brothers or sisters (if you have any), but that's another story.

I think there are some kids who are able to compete without making deadly enemies, but other kids are always trying to prove something when they compete. Mostly they just want to put everyone else down and show off how excellent they are. Nina is different. She's a girl who is pretty awesome at a lot of things. She is great at sports. The other day some girls were playing field hockey, including Nina, who is a hockey wonder girl. She can score goals with her eyes closed. But even though she's so great, Nina acts as if she's just an ordinary player. She passes to other kids. She praises them when they play well, and she doesn't act like a big shot when she is a star during a game. She never boasts and she never puts anyone down. The other day, after Nina scored this impossible winning goal in overtime, her teammates surrounded her, all excited. And do you know what Nina said? She said, "We all played well, and boy was I lucky to get that shot." I think that's called modesty or something. That's how Nina always is, all the time. She knows how to compete and use good social cognition at the same time. Remember Dimitri? He's just the opposite. I kinda like Nina. OK, I like her very much. I wonder if she ever notices Jarvis the Social Spy? The thing is, I guess that spies are not supposed to be noticed—even by girls they like.

By the way, I learned something else by spying on Nina. She keeps doing nice things for other kids, especially when she thinks they're unhappy or feeling really low about something. Like the other day she was sitting behind me on the bus when her friend Emma sat down next to her. Even I could tell that Emma had been crying. You could see that look on her face. She sat down next to Nina, who quickly asked her what was wrong. Emma said her mom was really sick and couldn't get out of bed. Nina immediately said she would come over to Emma's house and help her cook dinner so that her mom wouldn't have to do it. Yup, that's Nina; she's so kind all the time. She is always checking to see if someone is sad or has a problem and then she quickly figures out how she can help out. And you know what? I bet a lot of times when people really like someone it's because they're super kind and don't just think about themselves all the time. That means one way to act right is to act kind. Let's go for it!

Well, we've talked about some big parts of acting right, but before we finish this crucial subject, we need to give Professor Levine a chance to feel important without competing with us kids or trying to control us. He will say some things some of us won't understand and some of us won't want to understand and some of us won't understand we don't understand!

• DR. LEVINE SUMMARIZES THE FOUR BIG *C*s •

If you think about it, kids who really get along well know how to act when there's a conflict with someone else. They are good at *conflict repair*, which might also be called *social problem solving*. All relationships have some disagreements or problems that crop up. The question is: what do you do about them without making them worse? Kids with good conflict repair skills know how to answer this question. Kids with good social cognition also know how to be in control of themselves without having to be in control of everything everyone else does. They're also good at working with other people, at collaborating, and they can do so without taking all the credit for everything and hogging all the most interesting tasks. And, finally, strong social thinkers know how to be competitive in a friendly way, without making other people feel too bad about losing or about not being the number one perfect all-star in the group or on the team. You can be quite sure that a student who acts right in all these ways is going to succeed on the social scene. Doing well with the four Cs is not the whole story of social success, of course, but, especially when you combine it all with acting and reacting right and with speaking in a socially acceptable manner, it can definitely help you to be a winner socially. You can enjoy other kids more and they can feel closer to you when these abilities get used.

I also should say something about Nina, the girl who is really a good competitor and also a very kind person. Nina has a quality called *empathy.* That means that she is good at detecting when someone else is feeling troubled; she is almost able to make believe she is that person who is suffering. For example, when she saw how upset her friend Emma was, she asked herself, "What would I want someone to do for me if my mom were really sick?" By asking and answering those kinds of questions, Nina knows what to do for people who are in distress. Being able and willing to have empathy is something that makes friendships work best. There's another good word that describes Nina and is an important part of acting right. That word is *altruism,* which is when you do things that are very kind in order to help out someone. It's actually the opposite of being totally selfish and only thinking about what's best for you. Nina is definitely altruistic and not totally self-centered, and that's one reason she is so well liked and respected.

"READING" SOCIAL INFORMATION

Thanks for being so patient, reader. Now that you have Jarvis with you back in your bedroom or classroom or tree or wherever you're reading this book, you won't be able to put it down. After you think about all this acting right stuff that Dr. Mel and I are teaching you, a subject you've probably always wanted to know nothing about, you will realize something that your never-stop-thinking spy Jarvis just figured out: to act right, you have to be able to figure out some things about the people you're with, such as how they're acting and why they're acting the way they're acting. It's also important to look at how people are reacting, as Levine would say. I think there are some kids who don't act right with other kids because they just don't understand the kids they need to act right with. Get it? You need to be able to read other people as if you are reading a very complicated book for English class. Does that make sense? Here's how I found out about it.

I did some dangerous spy work one day in the auditorium, where I noticed three kids walking down the crowded aisle. I don't think they even knew each other. All of a sudden one of them, Anthony, tripped and bumped into Sam and knocked him down. It was a complete accident, but Sam hit his knee pretty hard against one of the auditorium seats. When Sam got up, he looked furious. I mean, he was fuming like a volcano. "Why'd you do that, you dumb jerk? You think you can just push anyone around. You're a…" (the editor just cut out these two words that you can't use if you're trying to impress everyone with how polite you are). Anthony quickly said, "Sorry, I tripped." Sam walked away looking very annoyed. Poor Sam couldn't tell the difference between something that happens accidentally and something a person does to you to be mean or to hurt you.

But hold it, totally confused reader, here's one more example. Do you remember that girl named Uma who didn't get invited to Caroline's party, even though her friend Aretha did? You mean you don't remember? Then if you have nothing better to do, go back and read pages 137–140 again. Your ace, number one, brave, unbeatable Social Spy, Jarvis, called Caroline on the phone and asked if I could ask her a question. She said OK. I told her I overheard this conversation between Aretha and Uma about the party, and I asked Caroline why she didn't invite Uma. She said, "Jarvis, did it ever occur to you that it's none of your business?" I said, "Now that you mention it, that did not even occur to me, but can you answer the question anyway, please?" "To tell you the truth, Jarvis," Caroline admitted, "I totally forgot to invite Uma. She knows we're all good friends. I made a mistake. I really like Uma; she can be a pain sometimes, but she's also funny and fun to be with. It would have been OK to have her at my party." I thanked her for the information and wrote it all down in my notes. Isn't that interesting, reader, that Uma didn't read Caroline right. She assumed that Caroline hated her or something. But Caroline just plain forgot to invite Uma. Well, those are two examples of how important it is to figure out other people and how they really and truly feel—and also why they do the things they do. That will help you know how to act right with them. All that takes some heavy-duty social reading, doesn't it?

And here's something else about social reading, something I noticed when I spied on this kid named Rob, who sometimes can't get along with anybody. I used to think that he was what you might call much too weird. Now that I am the world's leading kid expert on the subject, I wonder if he might have a problem with his social cognition. How's that, Levine? I no longer blame kids for not getting along; I try to understand them. It's Jarvis the Social Spy, social detective, and social doctor. Anyway, there was this group of about four wonderful eighth graders (including me) sitting around a table in science class waiting patiently for the teacher to give out the magnifying glasses and dead worms and some very smelly bugs to bug us and to fascinate our

Often, the way you are going to act depends on what you believe the people around you are thinking or feeling. Social perception is your ability to figure out other people's intentions or point of view, so that you can act the right way toward them. In a way, you read other people (things like expressions on their faces, their body movements, and their behavior) as if you were reading a book and trying to understand it. Just as different students show different abilities in reading comprehension, they also have differences in their people comprehension! Kids with good social perception can answer questions like the ones in this diagram pretty well.

Some Typical Questions That Take Good Social Perception to Answer

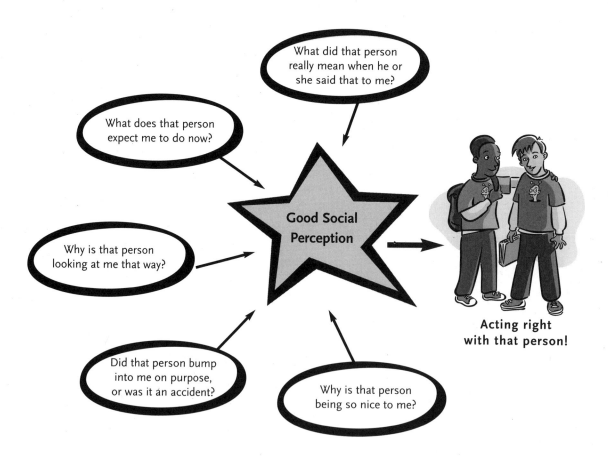

What did that person really mean when he or she said that to me?

What does that person expect me to do now?

Why is that person looking at me that way?

Good Social Perception

Did that person bump into me on purpose, or was it an accident?

Why is that person being so nice to me?

Acting right with that person!

hungry young minds. We were talking about this kid in our class who got put in the hospital the day before because she had a disease called viral meningitis, which they told us was a really bad infection of your brain. We were all talking about this and about how scared and worried we were that Ana could die or get brain damage or something. We were really scared and sad. Pretty soon, the teacher gave us our dead things to check out. Rob was told to sit at our table. He sat down and heard us talking about Ana for a little while as we were doing our worm work, and then he started joking around and laughing and playing with his bugs and talking about how he was going to put some worms in the teacher's coffee cup. He thought this was very funny and cool. But it sure didn't fit with our mood talking and thinking about a friend in the hospital. Everybody at the table felt really annoyed. Couldn't Rob tell we were talking about something very serious, that a kid's life was in danger? This was no time to be a comedian. But you know what? When I thought about it afterwards, I wondered if Rob is flunking social reading. Maybe he just didn't know how to read our worried mood and then act sad too. And by the way, Rob gets almost nothing but As on his report cards. He has OK reading comprehension but not much people comprehension! And I think I'm really right on because a few days later, there was a group of kids joking around at lunch, and Rob sat down with them and right away took out his math book and started studying and doing stuff with equations. He just couldn't figure out that everyone was acting funny and having a great time, and he stuck himself in the middle of the group and acted too serious by studying. Rob probably hardly ever does things that fit in with other people's moods. That may be one reason that other kids think he's a little weird. But Eastern Middle School's one and only Social Spy may be getting in over his social head. Let's call Levine to the rescue.

Social reading is sometimes called *social perception,* and Jarvis is correct. It's a crucial part of social cognition. Often the way we act toward other people depends on how we understand them. Jarvis gave us three great examples. In one case a girl, Uma, misunderstood why she wasn't invited to a party. In other case, Sam couldn't figure out whether someone tripped him intentionally or accidentally, And then there was Rob, who had trouble reading other people's moods so he could act right when he was with him. By the way, Rob was having a problem with what we call *mood matching.*

When we try to act according to our understanding of people and situations, we first have to decide how others feel, why we think they are acting the way they are acting, and what they expect from us. We look for many clues (usually without even realizing it). A person's actions and movements (sometimes called *body language*) may provide some important information. For example, if someone's body appears very relaxed, he or she is probably reasonably content and not about to argue or fight with you. In addition to reading body movements, we also need to listen carefully and tune in to what people are saying and how they are saying it, clues like the tone of their voice (does it sound angry or friendly?) and the words they are using (are they warm or hostile?) Then we try to size up the situation. Some kids do better than others when it comes to social reading. Uma, Sam, and Rob seem to need help with their social reading ability. So do many other kids who have trouble acting right. In most cases, social reading takes place so fast that you don't even realize you are doing it. This is because we all have plenty of practice every day all day long reading other people and figuring out their intentions and feelings. So this kind of reading becomes amazingly quick, accurate, and automatic if you're good at it. But remember, we all make social reading mistakes sometimes, and then we wish we hadn't acted a certain way. No one is a perfect social reader.

SELF-MONITORING: WATCHING HOW YOU'RE ACTING AND NOTICING IF IT'S WORKING RIGHT

It's Jarvis's turn, and I just had a genuine super colossal lightning- and thunder-filled brainstorm! I figured out that once you read someone socially and then behave a certain way with him or her, you have to keep your eyes, your ears, and your brain windows wide open to see if what you did worked. Brilliant, Jarvis! Hey reader, you know how Levine always talks about *self-monitoring*? I guess I'll toss in a word on that subject before he says anything else about it, because that's what my new social discovery is all about. We found out that you have to self-monitor when you talk, so you can know if you're saying something that bugs everyone around you. Well, in the same way, I guess you also have to self-monitor the way you act, so you can tell how that's coming across to the folks around you. Remember Palmer the Bomber? For a very long time he had no idea how good he was at getting people to despise him. That's 'cause he never noticed how they looked or acted when he was around. Poor guy. Hopefully, working with Mr. Ramirez will help him get better at self-monitoring.

Now it's time again for a brief (I hope) word from our sponsor who will try to impress us all with his final thoughts about the acting right parts of social cognition. I promise to reappear in Chapter 6 with some more of my thrilling heroic Social Spy stories. By the way, you only have forty-five pages to read until the end of this book—so pour yourself another nutritious glass of milk, make yourself comfortable, and hang in there.

• DR. LEVINE SUMMARIZES THE
DIFFERENT PARTS OF ACTING RIGHT •

I agree that this would be a great time to review the very complicated process of acting right socially. Let's just summarize the different parts of acting right. If you have good social cognition, here's what you do pretty well (most of the time, since no one's perfect at this):

AGGRESSION AVOIDANCE

SOCIAL REACTING

CONFLICT REPAIR

SOCIAL CONTROL

COLLABORATION

COMPETITIVE BEHAVIOR

SOCIAL READING

SOCIAL SELF-MONITORING

Kids who can meet these demands have an excellent chance of having a positive reputation at school and in the neighborhood. But these actions and words are much easier for some people than for others. If you have social cognition weaknesses, you might act in a way that turns everyone off or makes them think that you have no use for them. You probably wouldn't even realize all the things you were doing to offend others. That's a big problem for some kids. It's something they need to work on if they want others to like and accept them. Most of the time this kind of problem is nobody's fault. People are born with weak or strong social ability, just as they might be born with the ability to be good or poor athletes, musicians, or mathematicians. This means that it is very cruel to make fun of kids with social cognition weaknesses, because these weaknesses are not their fault. Of course, even if you are born a certain way, you can work on improving your weak areas, but it is hard social work. Even though some kids don't have to think about how they act, react, and talk socially, there are other kids who have to think about it a lot or else they'll make too many serious social mistakes.

We're now all set to go on to the next chapter of *Jarvis Clutch—Social Spy.* In Chapter 6, Jarvis turns his spying on himself. He will reveal some details about himself as he decides where to fit in, how to fit in, and how best to use his social cognition.

SOME SOCIAL QUESTIONS AND PROJECTS FROM THIS CHAPTER TO THINK ABOUT, DO, AND/OR DISCUSS

1. What can people do when they realize that they're about to do something that's too aggressive?

2. If you and a friend are having a serious conflict or disagreement that is making you very angry, how can you settle things without using either verbal or physical aggression?

3. What could you do about it if there were a student in your school who kept on humiliating you in public?

4. If you had a younger brother or sister who was part of a group of friends but was very passive, a complete follower who just did whatever they did (had no real social control), what would you advise him or her to do?

5. How would you handle it if a kid in your class were trying to take over and be the complete boss of a project you were supposed to be doing collaboratively?

6. Can you compete with someone and still be her or his friend? Do you think friends compete with each other a lot? What kinds of competitions do friends have with each other?

7. How does your social understanding of another person affect how you act or react with him or her? Can you give a few good examples?

8. When you are acting a certain way, how can tell if other people are getting annoyed or angry, or whether they are feeling good about you?

9. If someone you know walks past you without saying hello or noticing you, what clues could help you decide whether he or she is angry at you, really didn't notice you, was trying to avoid you, or was just completely out of it?

10. Are there parts of this chapter that would not be true in your school? What are they? Are there aspects of acting right in your school that were not covered in this chapter? What are they?

★ JARVIS PROJECTS FOR CHAPTER 5 ★

Writing Project: Hey, why don't you make believe that you would like to do some social experimenting to find out if it will help get more or better friends? Describe one or two of the following experiments that you might try (or make up some different ones) and describe how you could tell whether or not they were working:

• Collaborating on a science project with someone very different from you

• Hanging out with different kids

• Smoking or drinking

• Changing one of your activities (like changing musical instruments, starting an art class, or trying a new sport)

• Changing how hard you work in school

• Changing some other way you act (you choose it)

Spy Mission: Spy on two kids (one guy and one girl) who you think are doing really well socially, and watch how they act. Then make a list of all the ways they act that seem to help them make friends and be popular.

~ CHAPTER 6 ~
JARVIS SPIES ON HIMSELF

Hello there! It's Dr. Mel Levine leading off this time. I think that Jarvis has done a very impressive job of spying on the social scene at Eastern Middle School. We have seen how seeming right, talking right, and acting right come together to help kids fit in—or maybe even decide not to fit in— the way they want to fit in when it comes to the world of other kids. We've learned that there are some students who are truly excellent at doing what it takes to be popular, to have enough friends, or both. We know, too, that some students don't or won't have the language, actions, or tastes that can make them fit in where, when, and if they want to. Many of these students lack social cognition, the set of abilities that make it easier to relate to other people. There are quite a few people who are plagued throughout their lives by their own weak social cognition. It can affect their jobs, their social lives, and even the way they get along with members of their own family. And most of the time, people with social cognition weaknesses don't even know what social cognition is, so they are definitely unaware they are having problems with it. That's one reason why Jarvis and I decided to write this book. We wanted to help kids understand their own social cognitive abilities better and be able to figure out which areas may need some strengthening or regulating. Now that Jarvis has some experience with understanding social cognition, we thought it would be a good idea for him to think about his social life and describe to his readers how he sees his own social cognition at work. In doing this, he will also tell us some things that have happened to him along the way on the social scene. Take it away, Jarvis. I'll be back at the end of your chapter.

JARVIS TELLS HIS OWN STORY

Reader, you have to understand, I didn't volunteer to write this chapter about my personal life. Levine twisted my arm and talked me into it. He said I'd get paid for this, but I still have not seen one penny. He says that a lot of people will read this book. Frankly, I think the only person who will want a copy is my mom! My loving brother said that he wouldn't read it even if I paid him. Anyway, let's get it over with; let me let it all out now and fill you in on the not-so-secret life of Jarvis Clutch in the socially life-threatening dungeon of Eastern Middle School. I'll also tell you a little about the Clutch home scene. Don't expect anything very exciting.

MY FAMILY

First, I have one mother, one hateful, spiteful big brother, and a German shepherd whom I love. I love her so much. She is my little sister—really. We have no father. He left us when I was really young, and we can't find him. I've been

told that we don't even want to find him. But, actually, I think I do want to find him. I need him, maybe just for a little while, so I can talk to him about a few things. I have never fully understood why he left us and why he never tried to get together with me and my brother. I'm not really angry at him, just mixed up about it. Maybe my hunt for my father will be the subject of my next book—if people ever forgive me for writing this one.

My mom is great. She works two jobs, tries to give us whatever we need, and is full of love for me and my extremely-hard-to-love brother. We don't have much money; I can't buy the clothes the other kids keep talking about. But we have enough to eat and stuff. Mom cares about me a lot, and I care about her a whole lot too. I worry about her all the time. She weighs too much and she smokes too much and can't stop. I think about what would happen to me if something happened to her. I'd probably have to go live with one of my worthless mean uncles and my spoiled brat cousins. Sometimes I wake up in the middle of the night and can't get back to sleep thinking about that. Now that I'm getting older, I don't do that as much. But I do worry that I keep letting my mom down. You see, I'm not a great student. I don't fail, but in just about everything I do, it is decided that I "need improvement" (who doesn't?). Levine says that I have a difference in the way I learn, but I don't know what difference that makes! No one has ever mistaken me for a decent athlete. I still haven't found anything I'm really great at (with the possible exception of this new talent of mine, social spy work, and it could be that I'm becoming a really good writer). My room's a hopeless mess; only a lit match and a can of fire starter could fix it up. I guess I'm not up for any trophies from the Department of Sanitation. As far as looks go, I'm not bad-looking, but I'm not being entered in any beauty contests either.

MY BROTHER JEREMY

Here's something I really need to get off my chest. I need to say a little more about my brother Jeremy because I think about him a lot, even though I hate thinking about him a lot. You see, Jeremy is Mr. Teenage Front-Page Rage. He does everything well. He is so cool; I think he's planning to come back in his next life as an air conditioner! His report cards look like some kind of computer error where the keyboard got stuck on the letter A. The only thing he needs improvement in is his kid brother! Comments from his teachers make him sound like an adolescent god or saint. Jeremy is handsome; the trouble is that he knows it. He looks like a life-sized cardboard poster you'd swipe from a video store. He is a great first baseman and started playing varsity in tenth grade (he's now in eleventh). Girls are all over Jeremy. He is a member of several social herds at Northern High (which got its fascinating name so people wouldn't go to Southern High looking for the people who are at Northern High. If our very clever and original school people bless us with a third boring high school, I don't have to tell you what it will be called). Jeremy is cleaner than a bar of soap. His room at home looks so neat that you have to wonder if it's ever been lived in. My room is totally different. Everything in my room looks alive; swarms of local insect life are my loyal and trusty roommates. They get fat on my partly eaten bedtime snacks that I store on the floor and underneath my bed. Jeremy calls my room "the Jarvis Dump."

Our mom can't hide the fact that she is totally proud of Jeremy. Whenever she talks about him, she lights up like a fireworks display on the Fourth of July. And then she also has this kid living with her whose name is Jarvis. He's OK and lovable in his own way, but he's nothing to boast to friends and neighbors about. Jeremy recently got his driver's license, which worries my mother because she says that he likes driving too fast. I think I understand why he drives like that. Jeremy has been so successful all his life that he thinks he can do anything. He thinks that he can push all the limits and get away with it. I don't know about that, but so far it has worked out for him.

Now, Jeremy is not a complete bully in school, although I now realize he does lead others in making fun of kids who have weak social cognition. So, maybe he really is a bully, a verbal bully. Jeremy gets plenty of bullying practice on his poor, innocent weakling of a kid brother. He brutalizes me whenever he gets a chance. I try to stay out of his way, but he calls me a dork, a wimp, a pig, a weirdo, and a loser. That's when he's feeling kind, of course. He also pushes me around physically; I take full credit for the strength of his inflatable biceps.

Jeremy is really into his appearance. Once I accidentally invaded my brother's home office, the bathroom, and found him standing in front of the mirror admiring every inch of his body. He had just finished one of the 147 two-hour showers that he takes every week. I don't mind that he hogs the bathroom because spending time in there is not one of my most favorite pastimes. I am sure Jeremy would like to own a calendar with a different picture of himself for each month. That's the way he is. You can see all the reasons I'm so un-fond of my big brother. Anyway, reader, I'm sure that you're smart enough to have figured out that there's a part of me that's also very jealous of Jeremy. And Jeremy has no respect at all for me. He's ashamed of his wimpy brother. Several times he has said that he can't bring friends home because of me, my filthy bedroom, and my gross habits.

You know, deep down I think that my mom wishes she had two Jeremys instead of a Jeremy and a Jarvis. She would never say that, but I know she thinks it. I don't know why she'd want another Jeremy, especially since I believe with good reason that my brother is as real as counterfeit money. That's real enough for Jeremy. Even though I think he's a total poser, the posing seems to work for him. He's definitely popular. And you know, sometimes I think adults don't understand how much brothers and sisters influence each other. A guy like me has to figure out how much he wants to be like his brother, or at least *try* to be like his brother, or how much he wants to be his own person, even if being his own person is really hard. Don't all kids compete with their brothers and sisters? Probably the only kids who don't are only kids. But I bet that they sometimes have some problems because they can't practice their social cognition on their brothers or sisters. Look at the chart below that I made to show the differences between Jeremy and me. I gave it to my brother, but he threw it at me without even looking at it.

CHARACTERISTIC	JEREMY	JARVIS
Athletic Ability	Excellent	None
Physical Appearance	Very handsome, neat	Just OK, sloppy
Social Status	Popular	Controversial, some friends
Talking Right	Excellent	Good
Acting Right	Excellent	Very good
Seeming Right	Excellent—very cool	Eccentric—mostly uncool
Grades in School	Excellent	Average
Interests	Common	Unusual

See why I can't stop comparing myself to my "perfect" brother?

MY ECCENTRIC SELF

As you can see, I consider myself to be what you might call a little on the eccentric side. For example, I am the proud owner and stepfather of two teenage reticulated pythons named Walter and Elaine. Walter is about six feet long and three inches wide and extra slick; Elaine is a little smaller, skinnier and not as sleazy a snake as Walter. Also, Elaine definitely has better social cognition. I know that she acts right and seems right, but I can't be sure that she talks right! I spend a lot of time hanging out with my snakes. I really like reptiles and other animals like that, so on weekends I work in a large pet store, feeding the fish and the snakes. I have a friend, Tom, who is also into snakes. He has three of them, including one very loving, hugging boa constrictor named Sam. I have been trying to buy Sam from Tom. I'm still saving up. We also have a friend named Joanna who has a five-foot-long monitor lizard, three humongous tortoises (which look as if they were here when the world got started), and an iguana that walks on a leash and sleeps in her bed at night. Joanna's my kind of girl. To me, she's cool. But the kindly and sweet female humans at school have no use for Joanna. They won't go near her. They call her a freak and names like "Joanna of the Jungle" (and much worse). She's kind of more like a lot of boys than a girl, and she never talks about boys and stuff you put on your face and clothes and that sort of stuff that a lot of girls at Eastern Middle School find so 100 percent fascinating. Since she doesn't like talking about all that stuff, Joanna gets teased pretty often, is entirely rejected, and sent off by the other girls to social solitary confinement. I think she's cool, though, and I really like her. Sometimes she and Tom and I do things together. A few weeks ago we went to a snake and lizard show at the fairgrounds. I guess that's like some "normal" kids going to a rock concert or something. You know, reader, I don't think that you score a lot of social points at our school by being seen at a reptile convention. But I'm glad that I've been able to find some friends who are like me, and that we get along very well and have good times together. And we can be our real selves when we're together, even if most others think we seem anything but cool.

MY ATTEMPTS AT POPULARITY

First, let me say that I am not unpopular even though I do go to reptile shows. I don't get rejected, and I think that most kids who know me kinda like me, at least a little. Everyone thinks I'm funny. I'm known for cracking up everybody in my classes; I can even get my teachers to laugh at the comments I make once in a while during deadly serious, deadly dull class discussions. But I have to tell you that in the past, I tried to be more popular than I am. I made some attempts to be more of an "in" citizen at Eastern. Basically, I have pretty OK social cognition (at least in my opinion), but I guess I choose to be a little different. I think I pretty much know how to talk right. I don't seem to turn people off with what I say or how I say it. I can also act right. I'm not too bossy. I don't ever boast or brag. I don't fight with other kids (I'd lose) or argue a lot (even though I could probably win most of the time). I'm also pretty awesome at patching up conflicts and I have no trouble working with others—like on totally useless social studies projects and other assignments we get tortured with. However, every once in a while, I decide that I need to be more like my brother, more like the top popular kids at Eastern. I start to wonder if I can do it, if I can become popular. So I decided to start an experiment in popularity. Here's what's happened late last year when your friend Jarvis got his very long and narrow feet in the door that leads to popularity and social fame at Eastern Middle School.

Around last April, some girls told me that they thought I was cute. Now, I've been called a lot of things and I've thought of myself in different ways, but somehow the word *cute* never made it on the list. I mean, I think my pythons are cute; I don't know what these snakes say to each other about me. Anyway, because it was decided that I was cute at the beginning of that treacherous time of life grown-ups call puberty (I can't stand that word because it's just a secret code for getting hair on your body which is slightly gross and nobody else's business), your Social Spy started getting invited to some parties on weekends. His well-shampooed, in-love-with-himself big brother, who thought he owned the local partygoer franchise, was shocked that anyone would invite his unsanitary, nonathletic, unhandsome (but, of course, *cute*), uncool, weird kid brother to anything but the funeral and solemn burial of their pet ferret. Now reader, I have to assure you that these were not parties given by the top-of-the-heap, most popular, most admired, and most politically feared kids in the school. They were kind of the second shelf of parties given by OK kids, but not the Eastern celebrities (like Jeremy's fan club at the high school).

Anyway, I started going to these parties. I think I went to three or four of them. My mom thought it was cute, which seemed to fit, since I was there because I was cute. What was cute about me, I wondered? I didn't have a beautiful nose (a cute snoot). I didn't dress well (in a cute suit). I wasn't muscular (not a cute brute). See how clever I am? According to my English teacher, I have great potential as a writer, even though half the time she can't decipher my spelling. I keep wanting to tell her she has great potential as a speller! Anyway, here's what I learned about parties and about myself when I attended these parties.

I mastered the Eastern Middle School party routine pretty quickly. First off, I never went to any party by myself, because that would have been scary and totally anti-cool. When I got to a party, I would kind of go around and say something to each kid. It didn't matter what I said, but I had to make contact. Pretty smart, huh? Then I'd spend more time talking to just a few kids. Since I could never figure out what to say, I just pretty much said what they were saying. Now that I know so much about social cognition, I can say that I found out that I was great at code switching but not so good at topic selection. A lot of the talk was 100 percent pure gossip about somebody who wasn't at the party. I could never tell if what people were saying was true or not, but I thought it was most likely all made up or exaggerated. On the way home from the first party I went to, I tried to think up some new gossip rumors, really nasty ones, but I found that I wasn't so good at that. I guess I need practice. I thought most of the gossip was completely dumb. So what? At least it gave everybody something to talk about. Still, I felt sorry for the kids everyone was gossiping about. They could really get their reputations messed up. And what if they found out about the gossip? That could wipe out all their self-esteem (remember that word?) and get them feeling sad, scared, and mad. A lot of times, little groups of kids told stories about things in school or about what happened at other parties they'd been to. And you know what I found out? After a few of these social shows, I noticed that they were telling the exact same stories over and over and over again, although things got a little more exaggerated each time. But that made it more fun. Besides, usually the music was playing so loudly that you couldn't hear the stories too well, so it took a lot of time to realize that you had already heard them before, or at least stories pretty much like them. By the time you realized that you had heard the story before, it was almost over, but the music wasn't. Several subjects came up over and over at the parties, and I started to keep count. Here's the Jarvis Clutch *Most Popular Party Topics of the Year* list:

- Other kids (mostly gossip about the opposite sex)
- Sports
- Teachers that we can't stand
- Drugs
- Parents who hassle us
- Clothes

Boy, drugs sure came up a lot. I don't know how much these kids actually used drugs, but they loved to talk drug talk. I always left the parties early because I get tired early and like to go to sleep. Maybe they got into drugs after I left. I was never offered any—I couldn't have afforded the stuff anyway. Besides, the thought makes me a little sick. A lot of kids have told me that people have tried to get them to take drugs, and they almost have—just to be part of the social scene. But then I guess they figured out what a killer of your mind and your body and your life drugs can be, so they figured out better ways to be sociable. There are a ton of kids at Eastern who are popular and who are not going to let themselves get sucked into drugs.

When kids at these parties aren't talking, they're dancing. One time a girl asked me to dance. I told her I didn't know how. She wanted me to dance with her anyway. I told her I had to leave to go to another party (another in a series of highly creative, prizewinning Jarvis lies). Then I left. I'm too clumsy to dance, and I didn't want all those kids laughing at me and then telling their older brothers and sisters about it, who would then tell my brother Jeremy, who would then advertise it to my mother at breakfast. And then she might say that's cute. There's that word again! That would be horrible!

During party number three, I decided that in a way I was back at the reptile show. Everywhere I went, kids were displaying themselves just like some king cobra spreading out its hood or showing-off its fancy fangs. Every move of their bodies was an attempt to look, act, and of course seem cool. Mostly, I guess, it was the ways the kids sat in chairs (or even on the floor), or kept their legs in all kinds of special showing-off positions. They had their legs stretched out, spread out, or folded up just right, which I guess was supposed to let us all know how comfortable they were being at an important party. I thought they were mostly big-time posers. But you know something, reader? These kids were having a lot of fun, tons of fun. I mean, they looked really very happy and relaxed, as if they never wanted the party to end so they wouldn't ever have to go back to their parents (who give lectures), or their teachers (who just dish out assignments, tests, and grades), or even their big brothers and sisters (who act superior to them). Yes, these party freaks were about as happy as we get during our "early adolescent years" (a disrespectful phrase my health teacher uses to look down on us). They felt powerful, protected, wanted, respected, and liked (maybe even loved) all at the same time that they were having a ball. What a great package deal! But I honestly

have to report something to you. I feel a little ashamed to say this. I wasn't having fun. I felt weak, very phony, nervous, a little scared, and more like an outsider than someone who is really wanted and liked. Oh, I guess the other kids liked me OK, but I didn't like them, at least I didn't like any of them the way they were acting at the parties. No one seemed really real to me. It's like they were all acting in some crummy movie—posing and talking like some kind of movie script. And I didn't like myself there. I could never figure out what I should say, how I should act, and what I should seem to be in order to fit in. I have a very hard time posing. I just can't do it. I hate it. You'll never find Jarvis on the movie screen. The whole idea of pretending to be some-one you're not kind of freaks me out. There was a big part of me that didn't even care about fitting in, and yet a little part of me did. Life's so confusing.

Party number four ended once and for all my illustrious career as a party boy, and my make-a-go-for-popularity campaign. That's OK because, coinci-dentally, I stopped getting invited to parties. Maybe I started to get less cute—oily skin can do that to you (I've thought about maybe getting a skin transplant). Or else, it could be that the other kids could tell that I was bored and didn't fit in at those parties. No one could have accused me of being the life of the party! But the invitations stopped arriving, which is OK, since I would have used my remarkable creative talent to invent some excuses not to go to any of them. For now I'm back to snakes and just a few close eccen-tric friends like me. And Jeremy doesn't have to worry about sharing the telephone line anymore; it only rings for him these days.

Don't get me wrong, you party-loving readers, I don't dislike or look down on the kids who fit in at these parties and have the time of their lives there.

That's fine for them; it just isn't right for me, Jarvis Clutch. Maybe next year I'll start up my party-going work again; I'll have to decide. The thing is, there are a number of girls I see (from a distance) at Eastern Middle School that I would like to get to know better. They seem really smart, and thinking about them stirs up some chemicals inside of me—if you know what I mean. I'm trying to figure out how to get to know them better, or at least one of them.

MY LIFE AS A STUDENT LEADER

This year in school I have become president of the science club, which makes me the powerful and fearless leader of eight very inactive members. I was elected unanimously, but you should know that I was the only candidate. I also handle the lighting for the school plays, and sometimes I do the sound, too. Other students say that these are jobs for the local geeks, but I like doing them. I am also a fearless reporter for the *Eastern Middle School News* (another original local title). As you might have guessed, my articles are funny. My monthly column pokes fun at everything I can think of—even the newspaper itself. My latest sassy essay was a tribute to our cafeteria, which smells like cheese that has been cooked and recooked since the school kitchen was built forty-five years ago. By the way, the same kind of cheese gets used on the pizza, inside the ravioli, as a sauce for the macaroni, on top of the cheeseburgers, in the grilled cheese sandwiches, and I'm pretty sure in the gross-smelling wax they use on the floors. Because of the school's strong devotion to ravioli and its role in the lives of early teens, I have suggested we rename our beloved place of learning Eastern *Noodle* School.

Kids have started to realize that I'm very funny and that I'm different from them in some ways that I think are pretty unimportant. I don't dress quite right. I just wear whatever's around (blindly chosen from the garbage pile on the floor of my bedroom). The bathroom mirror belongs to my brother, not me. It's his most prized possession. I listen to classical music—Mozart and stuff—oh no! Whenever I try to put on my music, my brother turns his music up so loud that I can't hear my own thoughts. I actually like the music other kids listen to. I like all kinds of music, but I especially like classical music.

Actually, I forgot to tell you that I play a musical instrument, the cello. That's one of the reasons I like classical music so much. I think I am great at it and I have been writing some of my own slightly strange cello music, which is fun. No one has invited me to play the cello at his or her sweet sixteen party or in the marching band at a football game, but I won two little prizes for solos in orchestra. Other kids don't seem to care too much that I play the cello. Jeremy says that I should be playing the guitar. By the way, Elaine and Walter are my biggest fans. Those pythons are total cello freaks, and additionally how I dress doesn't matter to them, probably because they just wear the same scaly clothes all the time.

MY ATTEMPTS TO BECOME JARVIS THE JOCK

Unlike Mr. Perfectly Perfect, the god who unfortunately lives with me, I can't catch or throw a ball they way you're supposed to, I can't swim, and I know nothing about major league or college sports. I always get chosen last for teams, and yes, as I'm sure you remember, my kind, loving, and caring teammates in P.E. sometimes call me Jarvis *Klutz*. But in seventh grade, I decided that I needed to be a shining sports star in order to be a true honored citizen of Eastern Middle School's "community." I tried to find a sport that didn't require you to throw a ball. Somebody told me about cross-country running, so I joined the team. I've always been a fast runner. For cross-country, all I had to do was run a couple of miles in the woods and then run across the finish line. That takes some energy, *endurance* as they say, but that's about all—no balls to throw, catch, hit, or kick. I wasn't too bad, and I liked looking for salamanders and black snakes in the woods during the races. But then one day, a kid from another school passed me in the woods (not that getting passed by another runner was too unusual during my brief career as a cross-country star). The kid cursed at me and then he spat right on my sweaty gray Eastern Middle T-shirt. It smelled foul! I have no idea why he did that. I stopped and got a leaf and tried to wipe it off. Then I saw a big tortoise looking at me. It pulled in its head. It was as if it was trying to tell me something that I understood. It was wondering what I was doing in a track uniform. I was wondering the same thing. And you know, I realized that I would rather sit down on the ground and talk to that funny guy in the shell than run out of the woods and win some worthless ribbon or plastic trophy. That ended the illustrious, glorious sports career of Jarvis Clutch. I took my shirt off, threw it in a stream, and walked back to school. I realized that I wasn't really enjoying cross-country. I was just doing it to pose as some kind of jock. But it wasn't the real Jarvis. In fact, in P.E. I deserve an *A* for being the most outstandingly clever and imaginative kid in the class at custom-designing excuses for why I can't put on my gym uniform. My coach must think that I have asthma, arthritis, migraines, a bad heart, and some highly contagious life-threatening skin diseases that come out when I wear sweaty cotton cloth. The truth is that I'm very modest and don't care to have other kids seeing any more of my bony anatomy than they do when I am totally wrapped up in clothing. Sports and physical education just really aren't my thing. I need to remember how important it is for me to be myself and not try to become my brother or anyone else.

GOOD NEWS (AT LEAST FOR ME)

Now for some much improved news. Recently, my brother, Jeremy has started to be nicer to me. One of his best friends told Jeremy that he thought I was cool. I felt insulted when I heard about it, but that's OK. I'd rather be called eccentric, but at least his friend's opinion has made Jeremy start to treat me a little better. Jeremy has even started to boast about my writing, my sense of humor, and my musical talent to other kids. My very small accomplishments seem to be helping him out a little politically (unfortunately). My mom has noticed more of my talents recently, too. The other day she told me that she's very proud of me because I have the courage just to be myself and not be too influenced by other kids.

Now this project with Dr. Levine is about to end, and I am heading into ninth grade. That makes me a little nervous; it's gonna be hard to be a part of the youngest group right after I've been at the top of the heap in middle school. The other day I was thinking about high school and I wasn't worried about what my life will be like there. No, reader, I was worried about what *I'll* be like there. I guess I'd like to have more friends, and friends who aren't all just like me. I'm intending to work on that. But I still want to be the real Jarvis, not some kid other kids want me to be. Sometimes it's hard to know who you really are and who you're trying to be just to make friends and please and impress everyone around you. I hate that. I won't ever be happy unless I can be myself. I guess my number one assignment in high school will be to find out who I really am (at least for now). My number two assignment will be to learn how to go ahead and live the life of Jarvis. My third assignment will be to figure out how to do the second assignment while including, enjoying, and caring about other people in my life. That's a whole lot of work, but it's gotta get done.

Oops, this is getting a little too mushy and serious. You know what, Dr. Mel Levine? I think I've said enough about Jarvis, probably more than I should have. And I won't ask you to tell us about your social cognition because this book is getting too long, and, besides, the social lives of grown-ups don't make for good reading, in my opinion. But there's one more thing I have to do.

Now that I have finished all my Social Spy work (actually, now that I'm in the habit, I'll probably never stop watching and listening in on people), I have decided to offer some friendly advice to my friendly friends who are reading this friendly book about friends and are all excited that it's almost over. But first, yes, yes, I have to admit something it kills to admit. I, Jarvis Clutch—Social Spy, actually learned a lot from this so-called project that I was talked into doing with Dr. Mel Levine, even though it was hard work, and I have very severe allergies to hard work. I now think that I am the world's number one fourteen-year-old expert on social cognition, the social scene, social life, social death, and social fun. And now I am ready and able to help each and every one of you out there with you social survival. So read, reread, study, memorize, use, or translate this friendly advice into your favorite foreign language. And whatever you do, have a real blast reading the following list:

TEN PIECES OF SOCIAL ADVICE FROM JARVIS CLUTCH THAT NO ONE EVER ASKED FOR

1. Don't be too fake by trying to be too cool. Make sure you are not wasting your time and your energy trying to be someone you're not just so you can have a herd of admiring fans (instead of real friends).

2. Know all about social cognition and how it works (start by reading this book, of course). Learn the words for the things you need to do (like *code switching* and *conflict resolution*). These words help you think about what you're doing in the dangerous, wonderful social universe.

3. Talk to other kids about social cognition. Don't just take it all for granted.

4. Try to be part of groups that are not all alike. Find groups that encourage or at least allow kids to be different from each other instead of forcing them all to be the same.

5. Respect kids who are different or odd; there's a very good chance you'll be working for them some day. Being a little weird is good (I hope).

6. Find an adult you can talk to and trust with social questions and problems you have.

7. Don't bully, make fun of, torture, torment, or create misery for another kid because he or she isn't fitting in. Don't make fun of people for things they can't help (like problems with social cognition). It's OK to do some

teasing but it's not OK to cause major embarrassment (Levine calls that *humiliation*). That's just pure, plain, total, complete cruelty to humans.

8. Ask yourself whether you are paying too much to be popular. I don't mean money. Is your popularity affecting your grades, your future, your family life, your real self, or something else important that could hurt you badly later on?

9. If you have a weakness in your social cognition, get help with it. Don't just ignore it or think that it will go away by itself. Ask your sociable local doctor or someone at your school where or how you can find some help.

10. If you know a kid who is not fitting in but would like to, help that kid. That's what I call being a real hero (or heroine).

Jarvis's One and Only Diagram

Decide who you really are.

Then, go for it!

I can't let Levine get away with making *all* the confusing diagrams for our book. So I decided to make one myself. As you can see, mine's a lot easier to figure out. It just means: *DON'T EVER BE AFRAID TO BE YOURSELF!*

• LEVINE WINDS UP THIS CHAPTER •

Now that we have learned a whole lot about Jarvis and his experience with social cognition, we can move on. In the next and last chapter of *Jarvis Clutch—Social Spy,* we are going to ask you all to spy on yourselves to inspect your own social cognition. To do this, we will be providing you with a special survey you can use to think about and evaluate (that word again) yourself and your own personal social cognition. But first here are a few questions about Jarvis to think about and discuss.

SOME SOCIAL QUESTIONS AND PROJECTS FROM THIS CHAPTER TO THINK ABOUT, DO, AND/OR DISCUSS

1. How would you advise Jarvis to deal with his "perfect" brother Jeremy? Should Jarvis try to be more like him?

2. How should Jarvis get to know the girls that he kinda likes from a distance?

3. Do you feel Jarvis should be part of a group, or would he do better just having a couple of friends and doing a lot of things by himself?

4. What are Jarvis's strengths? What parts of his social cognition do you think that Jarvis needs to work on?

5. Do you think you would enjoy having Jarvis as a friend? Why or why not?

6. Do you agree with the advice list Jarvis put at the end of the chapter? Would you add anything or change any of the items on the list?

★ JARVIS PROJECTS FOR CHAPTER 6 ★

Writing Project: Write a letter to me, your friend Jarvis, giving me advice on how you think I should handle the social pressures of ninth grade. You see, I'm trying really hard to figure how I can be my own true Jarvis Clutch self, and still have friends and not be considered weird, even though a lot of my interests (like snakes and classical music) aren't the same as most other "cool" kids in his town.

Self-Spying Mission: Write or tell a story about spying on yourself (the way I did in this chapter). Talk all about your social life and how you see it. Include a couple of important social scenes, like when I described the parties I was invited to because I was "cute." Talk about how you felt and what you saw when you were in the middle of these scenes.

~ CHAPTER 7 ~
SPYING ON YOURSELF

It's Jarvis, who is very pleased to tell his readers that it is now their turn to do the spying. Throughout this whole overgrown book, Dr. L. and I have written about a lot of different kids and also about my extremely complicated, confusing life on planet earth. Levine (with no help at all from me, I am happy to admit) has designed a kind of a test for you. But don't panic, uptight reader. You will not be graded on this test. Probably no teachers will even see it unless you give them permission. Dr. Levine is calling this test your *Social Self-Spying Survey* or *SSSS* for short. Remember when we said that when you're a kid everyone keeps evaluating you? Now we're asking you to evaluate yourself—you can't escape. But this can help you—maybe. But it can only help you if you are totally, 100 percent honest when you fill it out! If you are honest, your Social Self-Spying Survey will help you think about the social part of your life and how you think it's going. It will also help you decide if you need to make any adjustments or improve in some parts of your social cognition. Then there's a section giving you socially curious students some ways of trying to fix up whatever you think needs some fixing up in the machinery we're calling social cognition.

When things are not going well socially, it can be hard to know why. You might want to blame everyone else for it. But according to Dr. Levine, you always need to check out carefully whether you, yes *you*, might be doing something wrong. That's what this survey helps you to do. So, get out a pencil or a pen or your favorite marker and remember to be totally honest, which you can be since no one will be giving you a grade.

• DR. LEVINE'S DIRECTIONS •

I want to repeat what Jarvis has said—there are no right or wrong answers on this form. There are only honest and not-so-honest ones! So be honest. You will notice that you can rate each item with numbers from the Key to show whether any of these parts of your social life and your social cognition are problems for you or whether they are actually strengths that you have. In the last two columns you also get to rate how important each thing is to you personally. You may find there are some things that are hard for you socially, but that aren't at all important to you. Of course, that's very different from having a problem in an area of social life that you consider important. Once you've finished filling out the survey and adding up the totals, then you should think about which ways of improving you might want to try.

It's Jarvis again with one last piece of advice. Unless some grown-up type tells you it's OK, you shouldn't write in this book. Grown-ups get all hot and bothered about that. But someone should be able to give you a copy of the SSSS that you can write all over. You can even find it on the Internet. Cool.

Now, go for it! Have fun spying on your own social cognition and trying to learn some things about yourself.

The *Social Self-Spying* Survey (Code Name: *SSSS*)

Name: _____ School: _____

Date: _____ Grade: _____

Age: _____

STRENGTHS AND WEAKNESSES RATING

1 = I have trouble with this very often.

2 = I have trouble with this pretty often.

3 = I have trouble with this once in a while.

4 = I never have any trouble with this.

5 = I think this is a real strength for me.

IMPORTANCE RATING

U = This is *unimportant* to me.

I = This is *important* to me.

Part One—Fitting In and Feeling Good about It

Social Part	Social Challenge	1	2	3	4	5	U	I
Popularity	Being popular with kids my age	☐	☐	☐	☐	☐	☐	☐
Popularity	Having a good reputation	☐	☐	☐	☐	☐	☐	☐
Friendship	Making new friends	☐	☐	☐	☐	☐	☐	☐
Friendship	Having a few good friends	☐	☐	☐	☐	☐	☐	☐
Friendship	Having a best friend	☐	☐	☐	☐	☐	☐	☐
Friendship	Having a boyfriend or girlfriend	☐	☐	☐	☐	☐	☐	☐
Groups	Becoming accepted by one group	☐	☐	☐	☐	☐	☐	☐
Groups	Becoming accepted by several groups	☐	☐	☐	☐	☐	☐	☐
Peer Pressure	Resisting pressure from peers	☐	☐	☐	☐	☐	☐	☐
Conformity	Not having to go along with the crowd	☐	☐	☐	☐	☐	☐	☐
Politics	Getting along with influential students	☐	☐	☐	☐	☐	☐	☐
Politics	Getting along with teachers and other grown-ups	☐	☐	☐	☐	☐	☐	☐
Independence	Feeling good when doing things alone	☐	☐	☐	☐	☐	☐	☐
Self-Monitoring	Understanding the reputation I have with others my age	☐	☐	☐	☐	☐		

Comments:

Part Two—Seeming Right

Social Part	Social Challenge	1	2	3	4	5	U	I
Appearance	Looking the way I want to	☐	☐	☐	☐	☐	☐	☐
Appearance	Dressing in a way others like	☐	☐	☐	☐	☐	☐	☐
Body Image	Feeling OK about how my body looks	☐	☐	☐	☐	☐	☐	☐
Movement	Moving around in a way others like	☐	☐	☐	☐	☐	☐	☐
Sports	Being a good athlete	☐	☐	☐	☐	☐	☐	☐
Other Skills	Having non-sports skills other kids respect	☐	☐	☐	☐	☐	☐	☐
Coolness	Feeling OK about how cool (or uncool) I am	☐	☐	☐	☐	☐	☐	☐
Coolness	Seeming cool when I want to	☐	☐	☐	☐	☐	☐	☐
Image	Having the image I want to have	☐	☐	☐	☐	☐	☐	☐
Interests	Having interests others share or admire	☐	☐	☐	☐	☐	☐	☐
Self-Monitoring	Watching how I seem to others	☐	☐	☐	☐	☐	☐	☐

Comments:

Part Three—Talking Right

Social Part	Social Challenge	1	2	3	4	5	U	I
Feelings	Expressing my feelings accurately							
Feelings	Understanding people when they talk about their feelings							
Boasting	Not boasting/bragging too much							
Listening	Being a good listener							
Conversation	Having back-and-forth discussions							
Topic Choice	Picking the right things to talk about							
Topic Length	Not talking too long about one thing							
Code Switching	Talking differently to different people							
Complimenting	Remembering to praise other people							
Requesting	Asking for things in a nice way							
Humor	Using the right sort of humor at the right time							
Humor	Knowing if someone's serious or not							
Output	Not having to talk too much of the time							
Output	Not being too shy to say much							
Output	Not talking too loud							
Telephoning	Being willing to call a friend							
Telephoning	Calling someone I don't know well							
Everyday Speech Use	Talking/sounding like other kids when I want or need to							
Self-Monitoring	Watching how what I say affects others							

Comments:

Part Four—Acting Right

Social Part	Social Challenge	1	2	3	4	5	U	I
Aggression	Not acting tough/rough/hostile/angry	☐	☐	☐	☐	☐	☐	☐
Reacting	Not reacting too strongly to things	☐	☐	☐	☐	☐	☐	☐
Conflict Repair	Being able to settle arguments/disputes peacefully	☐	☐	☐	☐	☐	☐	☐
Control	Not dominating or needing to be the boss	☐	☐	☐	☐	☐	☐	☐
Control	Not being too much of a follower	☐	☐	☐	☐	☐	☐	☐
Collaboration	Being able to work well with other kids	☐	☐	☐	☐	☐	☐	☐
Competition	Competing without too much aggression	☐	☐	☐	☐	☐	☐	☐
Self-Marketing	Not overselling myself to others	☐	☐	☐	☐	☐	☐	☐
Self-Marketing	Not being too modest or underselling myself	☐	☐	☐	☐	☐	☐	☐
Altruism	Doing things that help out other people	☐	☐	☐	☐	☐	☐	☐
Empathy	Feeling sorry for others when they're down	☐	☐	☐	☐	☐	☐	☐
Understanding	Figuring out why others are acting the way they are	☐	☐	☐	☐	☐	☐	☐
Self-Monitoring	Watching the effects of my actions	☐	☐	☐	☐	☐	☐	☐

Comments:

Using Your *SSSS (Social Self-Spying Survey)* to Examine and Improve the Social Parts of Your Life

This part of the survey is designed to help you figure out the parts of your social life that may be a problem for you and consider any changes you might want to make. First, look back over the first part of your survey and fill in the following information:

Record the total number of 1s, 2s, and 5s you checked off in each part of your *SSSS*. Since we want to focus on possible strengths and weaknesses, we will not pay much attention to the 3s and 4s.

Part One—Fitting In and Feeling Good about It

1s_____ + 2s_____ = _____Total number of things that may be a problem for me. Total number of 1s and 2s that I checked off as "Important to Me"_____ (out of 14 items)

5s_____ = Total number of things that I think are my social strengths (out of 14 items)

Part Two—Seeming Right

1s_____ + 2s_____ = _____Total number of things that may be a problem for me. Total number of 1s and 2s that I checked off as "Important to Me"_____ (out of 11 items)

5s_____ = Total number of things that I think are my social strengths (out of 11 items)

Part Three—Talking Right

1s_____ + 2s_____ = _____Total number of things that may be a problem for me. Total number of 1s and 2s that I checked off as "Important to Me"_____ (out of 19 items)

5s_____ = Total number of things that I think are my social strengths (out of 19 items)

·189·

Part Four—Acting Right

1s_____ + 2s_____ = _____ Total number of things that may be a problem for me. Total number of 1s and 2s that I checked off as "Important to Me"_____(out of 13 items)

5s_____ = Total number of things that I think are my social strengths (out of 13 items)

GRAND TOTALS

Please enter here the total number of 1s and 2s that you checked off on the entire *SSSS* _____ and then the total number of 1s and 2s that you checked off as "Important to Me"_____ (out of 57 total items). These are areas you might want to work on.

Next enter here the total number of 5s that you checked off on the entire *SSSS* _____ (out of 57 items). These are your major social strengths that you should feel majorly good about!

WHAT DO ALL THESE NUMBERS MEAN?

First of all, if you checked off every single item as 5, you probably have not been very honest with yourself, or else maybe you haven't examined your social life carefully enough, so try again. We all know that no one is socially perfect! Everyone's social behavior has parts that can use some attention.

Now look over all the 1s and 2s. Pay special attention to the 1s and 2s that you marked as being important to you. These are the skills you will probably want to work on. If something doesn't matter to you, then you probably will not want to work on it. However, if nothing's important to you, that could be a problem! If nothing about your social life matters to you, you could eventually have a lot of trouble getting along with others, which could hurt you in your education and in your career. This is your second chance to think over what's important and what isn't.

Once you have made up your mind what's important, you can see what you need to work on: those important 1s and 2s. If you want, you can make a list below of the social challenges you want to work on.

SOCIAL CHALLENGES I WANT TO WORK ON

1. _____

2. _____

3. _____

4. _____

5. _____

6. _____

7. _____

8. _____

9. _____

10. _____

Now that you've decided which social challenges you think need some sanding and polishing, you have to decide how to work on them. Read through the table below and check off the ways you think you might be able to work on your social challenges.

Ways of Working on Social Challenges

		I Might Try This
Goal Setting	Think about what you want to accomplish socially (such as maybe having just a few close friends) and then find ways to meet those goals.	
Counseling	Find an adult you can trust and see if that person can give you social advice and coaching.	
Modeling	Spy on some kid(s) who you think are close to the way you would like to be socially to see how they seem, talk, and act (what it is they do right). Try out some of their ways.	
Experimenting	Think of new ways you could seem, talk, or act. Write these down and try them out. Then observe how they're affecting others and how they make you feel.	
Interest Sharing	Find others who have interests like yours and get into activities with them that you all enjoy. Build social cognition while having fun!	
Self-Coaching	Develop a voice inside of you that keeps reminding you of your social weaknesses and strengths when you're with other people (for example, it might say, "Don't be shy," or "Don't hog this conversation," or "Don't try to act too tough with these folks"). Let this voice help you to make better social decisions.	
Confiding	Talk with a friend, brother, sister, or someone else you can trust about different social life challenges and the best ways to handle them.	
Record Keeping	Maintain a social diary. Each night review the day's important social events and describe how you did with your social challenges. Then write about what you might want to do differently next time. Rate your social success daily: 1–10 (1 is not-so-good and 10 is totally excellent).	
Evaluating	Find some kids who are having social problems and try to figure out what they're doing wrong and whether you're doing the same things. Then think about how they (and maybe you!) should be trying to make changes in seeming, talking, or acting right.	
Using Your Strengths	Think about your strengths and about what you can offer or do for others. Then develop some relationships by collaboration and altruism—helping others with your knowledge (video games, animals, or sports, for example) or your abilities (art, fixing things, or Spanish, for example). Use your strengths to reach out to potential good friends.	
Additional Ideas (of your own)		

Once you've worked on some of your social goals for a while, you can fill out the survey again and see if you've made improvement.

GOOD LUCK with your social improvement plans
from Dr. Mel Levine and Jarvis!

A GLOSSARY OF WORDS AND TERMS
USED IN *JARVIS CLUTCH—SOCIAL SPY*

Word or Term	Dr. Levine's Meaning	Jarvis's Quick Meaning	Page in Book
Acting Right	Behaving or doing things in a way that helps you get along with others	Not doing mean or weird stuff	125 (Chapter 5)
Aggression Avoidance	Controlling or stopping angry actions that are too rough and hostile and could hurt others	Cooling it when you're mad	131
Altruism	Doing kind things for other people	Helping others out	147
Body Language	Signals from your posture, gestures, and movements that give hints about your feelings	The vibes from your body or someone else's	152
Bullying	Trying to threaten, hurt, or humiliate someone	Ganging up on some poor, innocent, helpless kid	44
Code Switching	Adjusting the words you use and the way you speak depending on the people you are with	Fitting stuff you say with the people you're around	109
Cognition	Thinking processes—needed for figuring out problems, learning, and making good decisions	Brain work	14
Competition	Trying to do better than others—like in a sport, in popularity, or in other ways	Trying to beat out others so that you can look great	144
Complimenting Skills	Saying nice and honest things to people to make them feel good	Being good at praising	118
Conflict Repair	The process of patching things up when people disagree with each other	Making peace	146

Word or Term	Dr. Levine's Meaning	Jarvis's Quick Meaning	Page in Book
Controversial Kids	Students who are well liked by certain groups and not at all liked by others	Kids like me (for sure)	19
Cool	A word used by many students to describe a very good way to seem to others	That's also me (but maybe I'm the only one who thinks so)	84
Eccentric	A way of acting or seeming that is unusual and original	Being really different from other people	96
Empathy	Sensing the feelings of others and sympathizing with them	Figuring out how someone else is feeling	147
Evaluation	A process of analyzing another person's strengths and weaknesses	Sizing people up	65
Expressive Language	Being able to get ideas into words and sentences so they come out making sense	The way you talk	119
Fairly Likable Kids	Students who seem to be nice people but hardly anyone knows them very well	Nice kids . . . from a distance	19
Friendship	A relationship between individuals that is strong, lasting, and trusting	Pals, buddies, chums	27
Humor Regulation	Control over your attempt to be funny so that it fits in with the people around you	Kidding around in the right way	119
Lingo	A way of talking that fits with a certain group, such as the words that kids use with each other but not with adults	Words that are really "in," slang	111
Mental Health	Your feelings, moods, and behavior	How you act and what you feel like inside your mind	85

Word or Term	Dr. Levine's Meaning	Jarvis's Quick Meaning	Page in Book
Mood Matching	Making sure the way you talk and act fits well with the people around you and their feelings	Not saying gloomy things when others are happy and silly things when they're sad	152
Mostly Hidden Kids	Students nobody seems to know; they are inconspicuous, almost "in hiding"	Kids you never see or hear about—it's like they're inside the walls	19
Peer Pressure	Influence from others of your age that may strongly affect your tastes and actions	The power we kids use to get other kids to act or be like the rest of us	36
People Skills	The ability to be liked by other students and by adults	Knowing how to get along and how to play the social game when you need to	15
Politics	The process of dealing well with influential people in your life (such as teachers and powerful students)	Trying to impress someone or play them up so you can get ahead yourself	51
Popular Kids	Students who are very well respected and liked by a large number of other students	Students who are making it big-time in the social world	18
Popularity	Your reputation among others who are your age	How much most other kids like you and look up to you	27
Poser, Posing	Trying to make yourself seem like someone you're not (e.g. trying to be supercool)	Being a phony	88
Puberty	A time in life (usually early adolescence) when your body changes to become more adult	The gross years I am living through right now	73
Rejected Kids	Students who are not allowed into any groups and may be made fun of or bullied	Kids who aren't making it socially and who get kicked out of everything by other kids	20

Word or Term	Dr. Levine's Meaning	Jarvis's Quick Meaning	Page in Book
Reputation	The things that people around you are thinking and saying about you	How the world sizes you up	18
Requesting Skills	How good you are at asking for things without making others angry or annoyed	Using smooth talk to get what you want	118
Seeming Right	Looking a certain way and having tastes that somehow feel attractive to other kids	Coming across so others feel OK about you	63 (Chapter 3)
Self-Esteem	The feelings a person has about his or her own abilities and success in life	What you think of yourself	32
Self-Image	The picture you have of how you seem or your ideas about how other people view you	How you see youself, and how you feel about what you see	92
Self-Marketing	Knowing how to get others to appreciate your strengths and want to be with you	Showing off—but not too much	72
Self-Monitoring	Understanding how you're doing socially, so you can make changes if you need to	Noticing whether you're bugging others or doing OK	153
Social Cognition	The mind functions that determine how you think about and get along with other people	Your "people smarts"	14
Social Control	Being able to be with others without having always to be the boss or a complete follower	Having just exactly the right amount of power with others	140
Social Goals	Decisions you make about how you want to fit into the social world	What you aim for with friends and the rest of the social world	56

Word or Term	Dr. Levine's Meaning	Jarvis's Quick Meaning	Page in Book
Social Groups	The cliques or combinations of individuals that like to be together often	Different gangs or clubs or herds or armies of kids that hang together	17
Social Language	The ability to talk in a way that helps you get along well with others	Talking so your mouth doesn't get you into social hot water whenever you open it	99
Social Perception (Social Reading)	Reading what's going on in peoples' minds and situations to help you act right	Being a sharp Social Spy when you're with other folks	152
Social Predator	A person who seems to get pleasure from hurting the feelings of others	A mean kid who feels good when he or she harms, puts down, or embarrasses someone else	44
Social Problem Solving	The process of figuring out how to succeed or work out difficulties with various relationships	Deciding how to get along	146
Talking Right	Being able to express your ideas in a way that helps you get along with others	Sounding socially decent	97 (Chapter 4)
Topic Length	Talking about something for the appropriate length of time	Not gabbing about something so long others fall asleep, walk away, or think you are totally weird	117
Topic Selection	Knowing what to talk about, depending upon the occasion and the people you're with	Figuring out what's OK and what's not so OK to say	117